Praise

"In this thoroughly grounded book, Emmy Vadnais gives the reader a toolbox full of practical exercises for getting in touch with and effectively using their intuition. Highly recommended for anyone who'd like to advance beyond the occasional gut feeling and gain a more intimate and direct understanding of their full intuitive potential."
—Dean Radin, PhD, Chief Scientist,
Institute of Noetic Sciences, and author of
Real Magic and other books

"Our sources of inner wisdom are powerful and plentiful, but they await the proper nudge to unfold in our lives. In *Intuitive Development*, Emmy Vadnais provides keys to unlock this treasure. The benefits, she shows, are not just an increase in our menu of life skills, but also an abundance of joy and happiness as well."
—Larry Dossey, MD, author of
*One Mind: How Our Individual Mind Is Part of
a Greater Consciousness and Why It Matters*

"*Intuitive Development* is a masterpiece. The author, Occupational Therapist Emmy Vadnais, is a ground-breaking international leader in holistic service delivery. Her exquisite book is exceptionally well written, easy to read, and filled with a multitude of accessible resources and references. Emmy provides numerous stories that are relatable and replicable. Her descriptive knowledge is profound and serves as a stimulus for all readers interested in expanding their intuitive skills. This dynamic and insightful book leads the reader through hundreds of easily understood activities and self-reflective, contemplation moments designed to stimulate our intuitive abilities. I highly recommend *Intuitive Development* and will use it in all my Reiki, a Complementary Health Modality workshops for medical professionals and others. Reading *Intuitive Development* will open your mind to the endless possibilities of inspirational awareness and the connectedness of all life."
—Rebecca Austill-Clausen, MS, OTR/L, FAOTA,
award-winning author of
Change Maker, How My Brother's Death Woke Up My Life

"Emmy Vadnais's new book *Intuitive Development* offers readers a lucid foundational and pragmatic approach—almost a step-by-step how-to guidebook—to understanding ways to improve one's natural intuitive abilities. Vadnais does a thoughtful review of many different types of intuitive modalities, including psychology, meditation, martial arts, dream work, mindfulness, psychic tools, and heart-centered therapies. She includes simple exercises that anyone can do at home. Her book is a fun and easy read. I highly recommend it."

—Nancy du Tertre, award-winning author of
*Psychic Intuition: Everything You Ever Wanted
to Know But Were Afraid to Ask*

"Do you want to reduce anxiety, pain, and depression? Do you want to find meaning and purpose, happiness and peace, and develop a deeper sense of self-love and love of others? With a vast array of exercises and tools, Emmy Vadnais shows you how. Follow her on the road of intuitive knowing into the field of imagination, creativity, and dreams— where you will discover your innate ability to know yourself and to change your life." —Pamela Eakins, PhD, author of *Tarot of the Spirit*

"Emmy has been a courageous trailblazer in the area of holistic health for many years. Her book is packed full of practical techniques you can immediately apply to your life to enhance your self-development practice toward greater intuitive awareness, peace, and joy."

—Dan Eisner, OTR/L, Certified Coach, author of
The Clinical Success Formula

"Emmy Vadnais has written a tour-de-force, a compendium of the philosophy and many techniques concerning healing and intuition that an interested student needs to know."

—Bill Herbst

INTUITIVE
DEVELOPMENT

How to Trust Your Inner Knowing
for Guidance with Relationships,
Health, and Spirituality

Emmy Vadnais, OTR/L
Foreword by Jeffrey Mishlove, PhD

Love, Emmy Vadnais

ISBN: 978-1-7352632-0-5 (paperback)
ISBN: 978-1-7352632-1-2 (ebook)

DISCLAIMER:

The author of this book does not presume to offer therapy or advocate the use of any technique for the treatment of any specific mind, body, or spirit condition without the approval and guidance of a qualified healthcare practitioner. The intent of the author is only to relate her personal experience in the hope that it may help you in your quest for health and wellness. If you use any of the information here as a form of self-therapy, the author and publisher assume no responsibility for your actions. Do not listen to or practice any of the meditation or relaxation techniques while driving a car or engaging in any activity that requires your full attention.

The stories in this book are primarily compilations of the experiences of clients or students the author has worked with, and names of participants have been changed to protect their privacy. Some of the stories are wholly true and accurate, and in those cases the author received permission to include them.

An Intuitive Development playlist with meditations and interviews is available at Emmy Vadnais's YouTube channel at https://www.youtube.com/user/EmmyVadnais

Credits:

Heart painting: Emmy Vadnais

Cover design: Marieka Heinlen

Interior design: Mary Neighbour, MediaNeighbours.com

Photo of Emmy Vadnais, dedication page (opposite): Alexander Dixon

Photo of Emmy Vadnais, back cover: Kathy Van Guilder Photography

*This is dedicated to all who want
to feel at home with themselves.*

Contents

Foreword

*T*HE GREAT SWISS PSYCHIATRIST CARL G. Jung famously defined four major functions of the human psyche: thinking, feeling, sensing, and intuiting. Of these, intuition is the least emphasized and the most disparaged. For example, although we teach reading, writing, athletic, and arithmetic skills to our children, very little education focuses on the skills associated with intuition. This state of affairs, in my view, is a terrible shame—as intuition is the very source of our deepest understanding of ourselves, as individuals, and our each, unique purpose in life. The important skills featured in this book are generally never taught in school.

Of course, there are many forms of intuition. Some things come naturally, such as language learning in young children. Some come slowly, such as the wisdom cultivated over years of professional practice. Some lie below consciousness, such as the brain's amazing ability to perform calculations and analyses that find their expression in dreams. Some confound conventional scientific analysis, such as the empirical findings of parapsychology that, after more than a century, have finally been acknowledged by the psychological community.[1]

---

[1] In August 2018, the *American Psychologist*, the flagship publication of the American Psychological Association, published an article, *The Experimental Evidence for Parapsychological Phenomena: A Review* by Etzel Cardeña, summarizing the results of over 1,300 experiments with overwhelming statistical support for the existence of anomalous cognition.

In 1993, I was invited to assume the presidency of a non-profit organization known as the Intuition Network. The organization had been founded by Weston Agor, a professor of business at the University of Texas, El Paso, who had written several important books on intuition in management. Funding was provided by Lynn B. Charlson (affectionately known as "Buck"), the inventor of the hydraulic motor and also power steering. Professor Agor, who was stepping down, selected me as his replacement because of my background in parapsychology as well as the national media outreach I had by then achieved through the *Thinking Allowed* public television series.

One of the first projects I undertook was to establish an email listserver for leaders in the field of intuition—researchers, trainers, consultants, and authors. That listserver has been in continuous operation for the last twenty-seven years, reflecting the strong bonds that people working in the field of intuition have formed with each other. I believe that the work of these select leaders in the field of intuition is important because, as previously indicated, our culture is out of balance.

Over the years, I have been witness to many excellent books about intuition from all of these perspectives. In my estimation, this book by Emmy Vadnais ranks among the best of them. Emmy's personal story motivated her to pursue this path in life. She found that looking within enabled her to uncover an inner strength and wisdom, as well as a gift for synchronicity, which had been missing in her life. It saved her from falling into a chasm of deep despair, and even led to her marriage. So, for Emmy, this is a very personal book.

For you, the reader, this is a practical book filled with many excellent pointers and exercises. If you take them to heart, they will make a real difference in your life—just as they did for Emmy. If you are a student, a scholar, or a professional, you will find this to be a well-researched book beautifully augmented with the best references and endnotes.

From my perspective, the most important feature of this book is that it arose from an understanding of the basic truth that still confounds the scientific community. How is it possible, as has been demonstrated in hundreds of parapsychology experiments, that ordinary individuals are capable of receiving verifiable information from distant locations in space and time—with no known channel of information transmission? I believe the answer is actually simple. Furthermore, it is confirmed by the entanglement principle in quantum mechanics. Everything is interconnected. We are all one with the universe. This profound lesson is the basis of the world's spiritual and mystical traditions. It is the basis for achieving the peace that surpasses all understanding. In today's troubled world, I don't think any other message is more important!

Jeffrey Mishlove, PhD
Host and Producer
New Thinking Allowed YouTube channel
Albuquerque, New Mexico
August 2020

Introduction

*I*NTUITION PULLED ME INTO THE light, out of the dark night of the soul. It saved me from a life of unhappiness by resolving a crisis and several challenges in my life. It served me well at crossroads where I was confused and had to make hard choices. Intuition guided me toward answers that yielded treasure far greater than I had imagined possible. Then and now, it helps me to feel whole and complete. It enables me to live with meaning and purpose. It teaches me how to "Align with the Divine"— that is, live a more peaceful and joyful existence in harmony with my soul's unique purpose. It reveals to me the gifts I am meant to share. I would like to show you how you can do the same. The world needs your gifts.

I have worked in the healthcare field for more than twenty years as an occupational therapist and integrative medicine practitioner. I have also provided guidance and care as a mystic, intuitive healer, massage therapist, reflexologist, energy healer, healthcare education instructor, and writer. My intuition has guided me on an unconventional career path toward holistic, complementary and integrative health, wellness, and prevention care.

In 1996, I was a new grad, practicing as an occupational therapist (OT). After I had studied for many years, I was excited to begin providing therapy to people to help them be successful and as independent as possible with their occupations, also known as Activities of Daily Living (ADL). These include everything from work to play and leisure.

Occupational therapy was the most holistic profession in healthcare that I knew of at the time, because it looks at and treats the whole person—the mind, body, and spirit. This was before holistic healthcare and integrative medicine were as well known as they are today.

Within the first year as an OT, I became aware that for me to be able to provide therapy to people, they needed to be already significantly limited in their ability to function. I helped people who were experiencing a variety of conditions, including: cardiovascular disease; stroke and other neurological conditions, such as Parkinson's and Alzheimer's Disease; cancer; diabetes; traumatic brain injury; paralysis; amputations; and several mental health conditions. I longed to find out if there was a way to help *prevent* people from becoming so sick. I began to explore whether there were better, more natural ways to help them heal, recover, and cope with stress, pain, and suffering so they could live a more joyful and peaceful life.

I began to see that if I stayed in mainstream healthcare, I would not be part of the solution—to help prevent people from having to get so sick and lower suffering. I felt that stress was a major contributor working against health and healing. This was before studies showing that lifestyle choices can significantly impact health and wellness.[1]

Additionally, I was debilitated by the fast-paced setting and managed-care insurance guidelines that precluded providing more than 50 percent of what I had learned in school; the beautiful OT scope of practice I had imagined was, in practice, primarily a fantasy. Appointment time limits and productivity standards of how many people I was supposed to see in a day, the meetings I had to attend, and the never-ending paperwork were unrealistic, to say the least. I was just getting started and already feeling the negative effects of stress and impending burnout. I was anxious when working in some of these environments. Something didn't feel right. But I had been training for this for many years. Wasn't this what I was supposed to do?

Intuition and inner knowing began pulling me away from my safe, secure, and socially acceptable full-time job with benefits; listening to it, I moved toward a new, yet-undiscovered path.

Even though it was scary and I didn't exactly know where I was going, I knew I wanted to be on the other side of healthcare (or literally, "sick care"). Preventing sickness, helping people to stay well—that was the work I wanted to do. In less than two years after graduating as an OT, I embarked on a path of listening more fully to my intuition and what was calling me.

What if I had ignored my intuition?

I would have continued to experience tremendous anxiety, depression, and frustration for not following my heart. I would have felt I was part of the problem versus the solution.

What if I had stayed stuck because I didn't know how to create another way?

Same answer.

How did I learn what to do?

I kept listening to my intuition. Here's what it told me: I was drawn to learning about more ways to help with health and healing than were found in mainstream healthcare.

Following that initial pull, I heard about—and paid attention to—something called *energy healing*. Without a practitioner even touching a person's physical body, energy healing was reported to positively affect a person's energy to improve their health. Hard to believe, I know. But rather than answering my intuition with knee-jerk skepticism, I realized I wanted to see if there were any merits to these claims.

In 1998, I began a two-year program studying medical qigong energy healing at the first holistic health and wellness center in St. Paul, Minnesota. The chiropractic doctor and owner of the center had learned medical qigong energy healing directly from medical doctors in China. I soon began working at the front desk of the center and moonlighting at a restaurant as a hostess and bookkeeper to make ends meet. This is where I met my chef husband! It's amazing how the universe works.

I quickly became the manager of the holistic health and wellness center and administrator of the affiliated medical qigong energy healing school. I learned how to palpate and affect the energy along the same meridians used in acupuncture; however, instead of needles, I used my hands and intention with focused attention, meditation, and intuition. I received much validation from the people I served, and I realized there is more going on than we can see with our eyes.

This was the foundation for developing my intuitive healing abilities, each of which requires focus, attention, and the ability to listen to intuition. I was taught to sit in meditation to quiet my mind and cultivate my energy. I honed my intuitive abilities while training with a professional intuitive healer.

While managing the holistic health and wellness health center, I learned about the many benefits of nutrition, herbs and supplements, chiropractic, acupuncture, exercise, meditation, massage therapy, and other forms of bodywork. I began to witness healing in many lives, including my own, that had been adversely affected by stress.

One of the most relaxation-inducing experiences that I knew of was massage therapy, and that pulled me to massage and bodywork school. I became Board Certified in Therapeutic Massage and Bodywork as well as an American Board Certified Reflexologist. I started my own healing practice providing holistic healing, energy healing, and intuitive healing, and worked part-time as an occupational therapist, incorporating holistic healing into therapy sessions. I found this helped people's ability to cope and heal. I also completed more training in intuitive development, guided imagery, and meditation that further helped me support people along their healing journey and helped me in my own self-care.

In 2003, I became an Integrative Medicine Practitioner at Abbott Northwestern Hospital in Minneapolis—the first inpatient Integrative Medicine program in the world at that time. I determined the best integrative medicine interventions and provided services at what is now known as the Penny George Institute for Health and Healing. I attended patients on the orthopedics-spine, medical-surgical, oncology, cardiovascular, ante- and post-partum, neurology, physical medicine, pre- and post-operative, and intensive care units—as well as at the out-patient facility.

In addition to working with patients, I taught massage therapy, reflexology, relaxation, meditation, and energy healing to students, patients, caregivers, and healthcare professionals, guiding them to connect to their intuition. By accessing their inner wisdom, they lowered stress, anxiety, and pain, and several had more successful medical outcomes and quicker healing. Patients and staff quickly embraced these services, noting the benefits of reducing stress and pain. I helped collect data with each patient visit, and a research study followed. Results showed statistical significance of these services in helping patients have less pain, be more relaxed, and recover more quickly. Moreover, many of these patients required less medication, and some were able to return home more quickly. (Notice that this approach balances both logic and intuition—more on that in a second.)

In 2005, I returned to private practice, providing individual holistic healing sessions, consulting, classes, and tutoring. I now teach many complementary and integrative healthcare classes to healthcare professionals and anyone interested in these topics. In 2006, I began teaching intuitive development classes.

I have taught thousands of people how to connect to, listen to, and trust their intuition. My intention is that this book will do the same for you. Inspired by the content that I share in my intuitive development and integrative health/holistic healing courses, these pages can also be an intuitive workbook, if you choose to use it that way.

Intuition continues to be a great gift to me and the thousands of people I have had the honor to assist. I would like to help you connect with that deep knowing within you: your inner wisdom. It is always there, ready, patiently waiting for your attention. We just have to know how to be receptive and receive the messages.

You are already intuitive. We all are. Perhaps you were not taught how to listen to your intuition and trust what you hear. By learning the simple skills within this book, you will have a stronger ability to listen to the wise, all-knowing part of you—your intuition.

Intuition will help you to make decisions in all areas of your life for the best outcome, for you and others. However, you need to know how to listen. There are likely many times when you have listened to your intuition, but you may not have realized it. Or perhaps you have had intuitive experiences and would like to know how to develop your intuitive abilities more.

Ever since we were school children and probably even younger, we have been taught to think. We have been taught to problem-solve. We have been taught to rely on physical, scientific data to confirm our world and prove to us that something is real. While much of this is useful, our intuitive aspects have likely been ignored, and therefore, a very natural part of us—another way of knowing—has gone uncultivated and underdeveloped.

It is important to use our logical, rational minds. While intuition has its gifts, it needs to be balanced by logic, so it may be best to learn to have a balance between the two.

Culturally, we are in the process of transforming from being primarily materialistically oriented to being more loving, kind, and compassionate. We all want love, peace, acceptance, and joy. We need to discover how to support one another toward embracing this existence. Our very earth and environment are demanding it. This important aspect of our being, intuition, can guide us forward, creating clarity, understanding, peace, and a deeper connection to ourselves, others, and the universe.

Some of the greatest minds listened to their imaginative, creative, and intuitive selves to assist in bringing forward new ideas and ways of looking at things. Many great thinkers, inventors, artists, and visionaries allowed their creativity and imagination to spring forth in profound ways. They would often receive insights, messages, and solutions to problems in dreams. Albert Einstein, considered to have one of the greatest human minds, said, "I believe in intuition and inspiration. Imagination is more important than knowledge. For knowledge is limited, whereas imagination embraces the entire world, stimulating progress, giving birth to evolution. It is, strictly speaking, a real factor in scientific research." More succinctly he said, "Logic will get you from A to B. Imagination will take you everywhere."

It is my intention and dream that more people will be taught how to develop their intuition, that they will understand how they intuit and strengthen this inherent gift we all have. I would like to see intuition classes taught as commonly as logic classes are taught. Logic is important. Intuition is important. Both combined can be exponentially powerful.

It is often true that what you need to do is quiet your mind to be able to listen to your intuition. But if that were easy, more people would be doing it, and there are often more nuances to it than we know, hence the whole fields of psychology (study of the soul), philosophy (study of love), and consciousness (awareness). I present the material from a variety of different angles and perspectives for you to be the most successful in developing your intuition.

This book and the exercises offered will give you the tools to begin to trust your intuition and to access it whenever you would like. To get the most from this book it is recommended that you complete all of the exercises at the end of each chapter in the order they are given. This includes written explanations, meditation recordings, practices, and reflection exercises. Maintaining a journal is suggested for you to keep notes about the experiences you have with the exercises. Nevertheless, this is a book about intuition: feel free to let your intuition pull you to this or that exercise that appeals to you, regardless of order.

Please be patient with yourself. This is a gently unfolding process that requires investment in yourself and practice for your intuitive development. In a short time, you will discover what a wonderful asset intuition is, which will continue to grow, further encouraging you to keep listening to it.

Listening to my intuition led me to teach others to learn how to connect with and trust their intuition to assist them to be more healthy and happy in all aspects of their lives. Intuition has led me to write this book! My intuition has told me to put this out into the world for you. And *your* intuition has led you to it.

May you enjoy discovering and connecting with your intuition. It is always there, waiting for you to listen to it so that it can help you feel more fulfilled in all areas of your life: love in relationships and self-love; health and well-being; a sense of peace, joy, and understanding; finding meaning and purpose in your life and various life experiences; and feeling connected and at home within yourself—your body, mind, and spirit.

Emmy Vadnais, OTR/L
St. Paul, Minnesota
August 2020

1. What Is Intuition?

*Intuition is the ability to perceive or know
things without conscious reasoning.*
–WEBSTER'S NEW WORLD COLLEGE DICTIONARY

HAVE YOU EVER HAD A "gut feeling," a "hunch," or an "inner knowing" about something happening in your life, but you couldn't explain your impressions in rational terms? Chances are it was your intuition communicating with you. Our thinking, judging, worrying, and analytical, rational minds tend to dominate us, but there is another way of knowing that is always trying to get your attention, always trying to help you be more completely *you*.

This book will help you listen to your intuition if you can answer yes to any of these questions:

- Do you want help making the best decisions that will lead to more fulfillment and greater happiness in your life?
- Do want to have a clearer picture about why you are here, how to fulfill your life purpose, or how to bring your special gifts to the world?
- Do you want to be more satisfied and improve the areas of your life related to health, work/career, family, relationship, finances/abundance, or spirituality?

- Do you wish there were some wise being who could tell you the best choices to make?
- Do you want to find meaning, purpose, or a deeper understanding about why you had certain experiences—and how to move forward in positive ways?
- Do you want to learn how to connect to, listen to, and trust your intuition that is always there to guide you in all aspects of your life?
- Do you want to feel more peaceful and joyful?

Intuition is a beautiful part of us that is always there: our inner knowing or inner wisdom. It may be thought of as an aspect of cognition. However, it is not solely a mental process. In fact, it is beyond or different from rational and logical thinking. Consider it as a complex set of interrelated cognitive (mind), affective (emotion), and somatic (body) processes where there is no apparent intrusion of deliberate, rational thought.[1] It may be a way to receive the most accurate information.

The word "intuition" comes from Latin *in-* + *tuēri*, meaning the act of contemplating, to look at or look within, and the ability to know or understand something immediately, without the need for conscious reasoning or proof.[2,3] Other terms describe related experiences, such as extrasensory perception (ESP), clairvoyance, telepathy, psi, psychic ability, remote viewing, anomalous cognition, and precognition. For the purposes of this book, the term "intuition" will be used to include the above definition and the other terms that can describe a way to know or receive information that seems to occur beyond space and time.[4]

Research shows that intuition is an experience common to most humans, and it may be the most universal, natural ability we possess. A whopping 94 percent of the general public report having had at least one type of intuitive experience, and on average people reported having had eight different types of experiences.[4] Therefore, intuition could be regarded as an innate ability or unlearned gift that we can all learn to develop.[5] Many people believe intuition reflects our true selves. Connecting with your intuition may be like inviting this loving and full-of-light part of yourself to emerge and come forward—a built-in, unbiased friend who gives the best advice.

This great tool often goes underutilized, though it is a legitimate subject of scientific inquiry, with important ramifications. Uses of intuition have been applied to educational, personal, medical, and organizational decision-making, as well as to personnel selection and assessment, team dynamics, training, and organizational development.[1]

Someday we may see intuition classes taught in schools and universities, just as logic classes are taught. It is just as important to develop and has its own unique perspective and many benefits. There is no need to have any particular spiritual or religious leaning to explore and develop your intuition—although some find this helpful, and it may enhance your beliefs.

Intuition will consistently give you the guidance that you need at a particular time. After doing practices that will increase your confidence in listening to your intuition, you likely will discover that it is honest and correct, even if it doesn't always yield the answer you *think* you want. New, creative solutions may come forward and be applied in your life, displacing knee-jerk habits or patterns that may not be healthy or constructive. These new solutions will align with your core values, providing moment-to-moment guidance and empowering *heart-based living*—that is, reliance in all things on the wisdom, intelligence, and qualities of the heart.[6]

Intuition provides you with guidance on how to best proceed: which decision to make and direction to take. It helps you navigate your way for the best possible outcome for yourself and others. It is frequently acknowledged that intuition plays an important role in business decisions and entrepreneurship, learning, medical diagnosis, healing, spiritual growth, and overall well-being.[7,8]

Your intuition is always there, ready to be tapped, even during times of stress, great change, or confusion. It will help you make choices and provide guidance and direction when you have difficulty understanding what is happening or why it is happening—times when your thoughts can turn to worry and fear. Intuitive insights will give you a deeper meaning or purpose behind a change in your life or for an event. Perhaps you will suddenly be able to make sense out of seemingly awful situations. You may discover that what has occurred is for your highest good and greatest joy, and a benefit for all concerned. Or it may help you to create a better situation in the present moment or in the future by making choices that can steer you toward more positive outcomes.

Sometimes, you may be receiving intuitive impressions, but are not clearly recognizing them. Perhaps you discount or dismiss them. Your natural intuitive abilities may be well developed or latent. We all have feelings, hunches, and insights that may flash into our awareness. You may be using these abilities, yet uncertain about when the messages are coming through, how to listen to them, or when to trust them.

In modern Western culture, we are primarily taught to experience and understand the world from a physical, logical, and linear perspective. This is different from indigenous and Eastern spiritual cultures where intuition receives more attention and is often more valued. For more than a hundred years, the physical sciences have dominated in the West. With each new technological advancement, such as the development of the microscope that enabled us to see inside the human body and discover germs, the prevailing mentality has been: "If it can't be touched, tasted, heard, or seen, it doesn't exist." The physical sciences and logic are important, but they are not the only way to seek information or to understand our world. Intuition, just like everything in the universe, is a form of energy or frequency. Physics, as we'll see in a little bit, may also be well on its way to explaining intuitive phenomena.

We can't readily see thoughts or emotions, but we can feel them. We don't see love, but we can give it, receive it, and share it. Our intuition is similarly real but ephemeral, and it is always there, gently nudging us or waiting to be listened to. Is it possible there is a seemingly unseen world that is of equal value to the material world? Could it be as important as logic? If so, perhaps a synthesis of the two—material and intuitive information—may be ideal. When used together they may give us the most optimal way of understanding our experiences, making the best choices, and being in harmony with our life's purpose.

In addition to the five senses, intuition is a sense we all have. This is often referred to as the "sixth sense"—occurring in addition to or as a part of the "normal" function of the senses. As you will see, we may simply be using more or all of our senses when listening to intuition.

Intuition may be experienced in many ways, and everyone is unique in how they experience it. You may discover that one, two, or three of your senses more easily detect information when listening to your intuition. You may have feelings, a certain knowing, or your emotions may signal what may need your attention. Intuitive skill comes from increasing your ability to discern when it is your intuition rather than a projection of an emotion or some unresolved issue, for example: our hopes and dreams clouding our insight, or fears about the outcome.

Intuition is a connection with your inner self, which is why it is so important to quiet the mind or meditate. This will help you to listen within and receive information that is always there just below the surface. When your mind is more calm and quiet, you will be in touch with the part of you that has less judgment, reasoning, projection, and emotional incoherence. This calm, quiet state of consciousness is often referred to as "being in the flow."

When you access your intuition, you will likely experience a greater connection to something beyond yourself or a higher part of yourself, engendering a sense of beauty and peace. You may connect more deeply to your spirituality, and that can create better health and joy.[9] Listening to your intuition often becomes a very direct connection to your soul, spirit, God, the divine, the one, the all, the higher self, witness, true self, or the observer—however you conceive of it according to your beliefs and terminology. Indeed, some experience their very soul when intuition is present and alive.

Story

Gwendolyn, a corporate executive in the same company for ten years, had enjoyed her position and had been promoted due to her strong ability to see the big picture, exceed client expectations, and resolve conflicts. But recently she was having a difficult time feeling fulfilled, and coworkers seemed to value her input less on projects.

She questioned whether she was burnt out and if she should stay with this company in her current role, move to another position, or leave altogether, but she didn't know where she would go. Her stress levels were through the roof; despite constant fatigue she was not sleeping well; she experienced chronic headaches; and her stomach was often upset. She couldn't recall the last time she felt joy.

She sought my support to aid her with her health symptoms and making choices related to her career. To help her be more relaxed and better able to listen to her intuition, I guided her in abdominal breathing, progressive relaxation, and assisted her in a "special place" guided imagery. She imagined being at an ocean beach at dusk when the sun was low on the horizon. She imagined that she was resting on a beach towel with her bare feet in the warm sand. She could hear the waves gently lapping on the shore with birds singing off in the distance and felt the soft air on her skin. She enjoyed simply sitting and being. She felt peaceful.

Gwendolyn's special place was at a beach, but one can choose anywhere. For Gwendolyn, the beach was just what she needed to lower her worry, stress, confusion, and frustration. When we imagine having a pleasant experience, our minds and bodies can virtually not tell the difference between what is real or imaginary. This enables us to lower our *stress response*. The "fight, flight, or freeze" reaction shifts instead to the *relaxation response*—the "rest and digest" response that delivers many health benefits, including helping our minds and bodies feel calmer and better able to connect with intuition.

I guided Gwendolyn to her inner wisdom through imagining that an inner guide was coming forward—an all-knowing, all-loving, wise, and compassionate entity who could help her find answers to her questions about her work and health symptoms. She began to sense a loving presence and the image became clearer: it was her grandmother, with whom she was close when a little girl. She began crying. She had not seen her grandmother since she had passed over fifteen years ago. She was so happy to see her!

I guided her to say hello to her grandmother and respond in any way that was easy for her to understand. Her grandmother's name was Edith and she gave Gwendolyn a warm embrace. I guided her to listen to see if there were any messages coming forward from her grandmother or if she had anything to share with her. Edith told Gwendolyn, "I love you so much. You have been doing such a good job in your life. What brings you joy? Do more of that. Your gifts and abilities will be used well wherever you choose to go." Gwendolyn knew that meant slowing down at work, taking on fewer commitments, and spending more time taking better care of herself. Her grandmother said, "I am always here. Call on me for support. You are beautiful and loved. You deserve to be happy. Always love yourself."

When Gwendolyn was ready and felt she had received enough insight, I guided her to bring her awareness back to the room and open her eyes. I told her that she can always connect with her grandmother, to feel her presence for wisdom and support. All she needed to do was quiet her mind with a relaxing activity, take a couple of deep breaths, and imagine being there with her grandmother.

"That was amazing. It was so real," Gwendolyn said. I asked her how she felt. She said, "I feel peaceful, hopeful, and loved. I'm grateful to have been able to connect with my grandmother. It always makes me feel so good to be with her. I realize that I have been working hard to do my best, but I have forgotten about me in the process. I want to keep working at this company. Maybe if I take better care of myself and have limits with commitments, I can continue there. If it's not right to stay there, I feel okay knowing that I will find a place where I can share my gifts. I have been wanting to take a yoga class and explore more ways to be healthy."

Gwendolyn had a few more visits with me. She learned how to access her intuition and developed regular meditation, guided imagery, and yoga practices. Her headaches and stomach upset have been eliminated. She met with a nutritionist and has learned how to eat better. She sleeps well, has increased energy, and is more joyful.

Story

"I think you were the first person I ever took an intuition course with. I think what I found most helpful was just having permission to 'play with it' a bit and not try and get it right somehow. You also made it clear that we all have intuitive abilities, and it's just a matter of how tuned in we are at any given moment. Once I started getting my ego out of the way (the part of me that honestly thought it would be cool to be more intuitive and know the answers) is when things started to really unfold in a completely different way.

"Fast forward to where I am now, years later. I call myself 'intuitive'— not 'an intuitive'—and am really happy just letting it happen when it happens, not to worry when it doesn't, and to be in constant awe and amazement of the gift. Your spirit of lightheartedness about the whole thing is part of what has made that super easy—thanks!"

Much love!
Diane Dempster

Written Practice

When was a time that you had an intuitive experience? For example, when the phone rang and you knew who was calling. Or you were thinking of someone and then they called you.

- How did you know it was your intuition?
- What senses were activated during this experience?
- Did you trust it at the time?

Write your whole story—whatever comes, without judging or censoring. Put the story aside and then read it a few days later.

Experiential Practice

Listen to Abdominal Breathing: https://www.youtube.com/watch?v=KzFzMOlPfzc

Focusing on your breath is one of the first steps in slowing your mind and relaxing your body.

Bring your attention to your breathing, notice your breathing.

Diaphragm or abdominal breathing allows your lungs to fill completely, while your body and mind relax.

Sit or lie down in a comfortable position.

You may place your hand on your abdomen so you can feel where your breath is.

When breathing in, allow your abdomen to expand as your hand rises.

When breathing out, allow your abdomen and your hand to come back toward your body.

This may feel a little different to you than how you normally breathe. With practice, you will naturally breathe this way.

Allow your belly to rise with each breath in and come toward your body with each breath out.

It is helpful to begin any relaxation time with a few slow, deep breaths in and out. Diaphragm breathing is one of the most effective ways to slow the body down.

Diaphragm breathing allows for more relaxation as you are letting your diaphragm expand fully so you are able to get more oxygen. Also, as you are not breathing up in your chest, your shoulders and upper body muscles are able to relax and not work so hard, thus allowing the rest of the muscles in your body to relax.

Continue to diaphragm breathe during relaxation time in an un-forced, relaxed manner. Once you practice enough, it will become second nature to you.

Journal

- How did it feel to follow your breath?
- What did you notice?
- Write a journal entry about this.

2. How Intuition Can Assist You

*Your answer will become clear only when
you can look into your own heart.
Without, everything seems discordant;
only within does it coalesce into unity.
Who looks outside, dreams; who looks inside, awakes.*
—CARL JUNG

THOUSANDS OF CLINICAL PRACTICE SESSIONS and the many classes I have taught, helping people access their intuition, as well as my own personal experiences, have confirmed for me the validity of much of the research about intuition. I have observed many people derive tremendous benefit from listening to their intuition—it brings forward creative insight and solutions that were not accessible during analytical, critical, and often judgmental states of the mind. It's usually the skeptics who feel more research is needed to validate these claims. However, no amount of research will help a person understand intuition. To understand you need to experience, not just read about, the phenomenon. When you dive into this part of your consciousness you gain insight into creative awareness and solutions you could never *think* your way to. Fresh ideas effortlessly arise, and you can discern the best way to continue to evolve. Your best guide and teacher is often you—accessed by looking within. Let your personal experiences validate your intuition.

Benefits of Intuition

- Improve guidance and decision-making
- Connect us with wisdom
- Enhance life and relationship skills
- Improve health, healing, disease prevention, and wellness
- Give us a greater understanding of ourselves
- Strengthen self-confidence, self-esteem, self-love, and self-acceptance
- Augment compassion for the self and others
- Help us understand why something is happening and how best to proceed
- Give meaning and purpose in all aspects of life
- Assist us to be more confident, balanced, and centered
- Guide us to be more present and calm in our interactions with others
- Calm and balance anyone who experiences over-thinking, worry, stress, anxiety, depression, trauma, or post traumatic stress disorder (PTSD)
- Assist those who are extra-sensitive to discern their own thoughts, emotions, and energy versus those coming from others or the environment
- Aid with mental or emotional challenges
- Support healthy boundaries and facilitate healthy relationships
- Stimulate creativity and imagination
- Improve innovation
- Focus problem-solving
- Promote spiritual connection
- And more

Happiness and Peace

How happy are you? We all want to be happy. Research has shown that those who live in the present moment report feeling happier.[1] When connected to your intuition, you are in the present moment. Being in the present moment can help you connect with your intuition. I some-times refer to it as "no-time zone," where there does not seem to be a past or a future; just now.

The popular meditation and way of life currently known as "mind-fulness" comes from *Vipassana*, a Buddhist meditation that means "clear seeing"—and that is precisely what intuition is. It is being present with nonjudgmental and compassionate awareness, allowing thoughts, feel-ings, and emotions to come and go, without getting caught up in them. This can increase awareness, clarity, acceptance of the present-moment reality, and resilience. It can create a sense of calm and peace.

Happiness is correlated with health. Martin Seligman, the founder of the positive psychology movement, identified three components of happiness: pleasure (the smiley-face component), engagement (the depth of involvement with one's family, work, romance, and hobbies), and meaning (using personal strengths to serve some larger end). Pleasure is the least consequential. He says, "This is newsworthy because so many Americans build their lives around pursuing pleasure. It turns out that engagement and meaning are more important."

Seligman suggests that the best way to find lasting happiness is to discover your strengths and deploy them. Intuition can help you do this. He describes how the cerebral virtues of curiosity and love of learning are less strongly tied to happiness than the interpersonal virtues of kindness, gratitude, and a capacity for love. When you engage in appreciation or gratitude and kindness to others it can give you a lift. This can give more meaning and purpose to your life, because you're both helping someone else and feeling more connected to others.[2]

You may find that your spirituality becomes more developed as you are able to listen to your intuition. You may experience a connection to something greater than yourself rather than a sense of separateness. Your personal connection to the divine source or higher power—however you conceive of that—may grow.[3]

Clarity and Decision Making

You probably want to make the best decisions you can in life. Intuition will deliver this, both in the information-gathering phase, with actions or non-actions you choose to take, and in the outcomes.

Once you are more consistently connected to your intuition, you will more easily sense this wisdom, trust it, and receive guidance and direction. At the same time you will experience a boost in creativity and self-confidence, resulting in new learning, healing, personal development and transformation, and spiritual growth. You will have more clarity about what is right and best for you at a given moment. You may better understand the past and create a joyful and peaceful future.

When functioning from your intuitive mind, your thinking changes. You will see and experience the world with wisdom, grace, and love, engendering decisions that are attuned to life from a greater understanding and a more whole perspective. In Western culture we value self-expression of thoughts, preferences, and feelings, and intuition may help with discovery of our selfhood, unlocking a sense of freedom.[4]

Creativity, Problem-solving, and Innovation

Research has shown that intuition may be a critical component of creative thinking and problem-solving.[5] Creativity and innovation are priorities for organizations around the world. For economies and societies to be successful, we need to be creative.[6]

In his book *Hare Brain, Tortoise Mind*, cognitive scientist Guy Claxton states that many problems can be solved by using more intuitive thinking than logical processes. There is a common assumption that the quick-thinking "hare brain" will win over the slower intuition of the "tortoise mind." However, Claxton shares research on how subliminal perception, problem-solving, and creativity may come from intelligence just below conscious levels of awareness. He proposes that when we free up this intelligence and creativity and are less analytical, it may help us negotiate complex situations.[7]

Well-known mathematicians, scientists, and artists have long recognized that intuition is a key component to their creative process and necessary for their original methods and new findings.[8,9,10] Steve Jobs, considered to be a pioneer in technology, highlighted intuition at the core of his creative visions.[11] Intuition and imagination are necessary for knowledge creation, according to research in *The Role of Intuition in the Generation and Evaluation Stages of Creativity*. Intuition is frequently reported to be an integral piece of the idea-generation process; idea generation and idea evaluation are essential steps of creative cognition and creative problem-solving.[12]

Intuition can enhance creativity, and engaging in a creative activity may enhance your intuition. This can include anything you create, such as art, music, writing in a journal, poetry or a book, a garden, a piece of furniture, a satisfying meal, a family, a fulfilling relationship, your dream vacation, and so on. What you create may be a direct manifestation of your thoughts. When you are focused on something that you enjoy, such as creative expression, you may experience being in the flow.

Being in the Flow

When you're immersed in the moment with whatever activity you're engaging in, not thinking of the past or the future—being in the now—the subsequent flow can create the most exhilarating, joyful, or serene feelings. This, ancient wisdom sages have said for millennia, is the path to enlightenment. Modern healthcare research shows that this flow state may help people prevent, recover from, or cope with disease.

Mihaly Csikszentmihalyi says in his book *Flow: The Psychology of Optimal Experience*, "[I]n our studies, we found that every flow activity, whether it involved competition, chance, or any other dimension of experience, had this in common: It provided a sense of discovery, a creative feeling of transporting the person into a new reality. It pushed the person to higher levels of performance and led to previously un-dreamed-of states of consciousness. In short, it transformed the self by making it more complex. In this growth of the self lies the key to flow activities."[13]

Engaging in intuition and creative activities will likely help you feel in the flow. When you are connected to and listening to your intuition, you are in the flow. Intuition can help you choose meaningful activities in your life, inducing flow.

Peace and Relaxation

There are steps you can take to help lower stress and anxiety to help your body and mind return to homeostatic balance and connect with intuition; for instance, engaging in relaxing activities, relaxation techniques, meditation, and guided imagery. There is evidence that the more you elicit the relaxation response, the greater your chances are of preventing and recovering from disease. Your genes can literally change to a positive expression that is the opposite of the stress response that can create disease.[14] There are many ways to enter into the relaxation response and listen to your intuition. The classic way is through meditation. You will learn about how to have a successful meditation practice in Chapter 6.

Confidence and Self-Esteem

Your intuition can help you to believe in yourself. Intuition can strengthen a sense of who you are, what you're doing on Earth, and guide you to follow your dreams. After you've listened to your intuition and applied the wisdom you have received, you will likely see positive results occurring in your life, career, home, health, and relationships. This will naturally strengthen your self-confidence and self-esteem. People who constantly view their intuition as valid have more steady implicit and explicit self-esteem. Conversely, those who have lower faith in their intuition have a negative relationship with their self-esteem.[15]

Self-Love and Acceptance

Your intuition can help you move toward loving and accepting yourself. Learning to appreciate yourself and practicing self-love and self-acceptance may help you to feel better about everything. Appreciating and valuing yourself will help you to see and understand yourself better. Go ahead, say, "Thank you!" to *you*. Being more compassionate with yourself, and forgiving yourself, will help you to be more grateful, kind, and gentle and move toward forgiveness of yourself and others. It may help you to engage in meaningful and enjoyable activities that can help you to feel more grateful. This can help you feel happier.[2]

Increasing confidence, self-esteem, self-love, self-acceptance, and feeling more balanced and centered within, additionally may help with mental or emotional challenges, calming and balancing those who experience over-thinking, worry, stress, anxiety, depression, trauma, or PTSD. You may find you can do much of this on your own, while professional help can further assist to transform any limiting beliefs you hold about yourself.

Gratitude and Kindness

What are you grateful for? Your intuition may help you see more clearly what you are grateful for and it may help you feel gratitude. Taking a few moments each day or week to have an attitude of gratitude may improve your life. When you are in a grateful state, you can more easily access your intuition. As you gain clarity about the direction to take in life, more meaning, and deepened understanding, you will naturally feel grateful about what is happening in your life and the course you choose to take. There is a correlation between gratitude and an overall sense of well-being.[16]

Focus on What's Right

Intuition can help you to focus on what is right in your life. And likewise, when you're in a more positive state, you may sense your intuition with less effort. It may seem easier to focus on what you feel is going "wrong" or what you want to improve. Doing so can help you clarify what you want to improve so you can make a goal and plan on how to achieve it. For survival, humans are wired to worry, but you can free yourself from states of fear, worry, pain, or depression.[17]

Focusing on what's right elicits gratitude and facilitates access to intuition. Hence, you likely will feel kinder and may engage in activities that are more altruistic. This can improve happiness. Robert Emmons, a psychologist, found that gratitude can improve physical health, raise energy levels, and for patients with neuromuscular disease, relieve pain and fatigue. Doing five acts of kindness (eliciting your gratitude) a week can measurably boost happiness.[2]

Giving can make you feel good about yourself. According to Mihaly Csikszentmihalyi:

> When you're volunteering, you're distracting your-self from your own existence, and that's beneficial. More fuzzily, giving puts meaning into your life. You have a sense of purpose because you matter to someone else. Almost every person feels happier when they're with other people. . . . It's paradoxical because many of us think we can hardly wait to get home and be alone with nothing to do, but that's a worst-case scenario. If you're alone with nothing to do, the quality of your experience really plummets.[2]

> *Gratitude is the appreciation of what is valuable*
> *and meaningful to oneself and represents a general*
> *state of thankfulness and/or appreciation.*
> —SANSONE & SANSONE, 2010

Experiencing gratitude, joy, and peacefulness may help you to be in the physiological state of the *relaxation response*, explained more in Chapter 6. There is strong evidence that this assists in generating positive psychological states, recovering from illness, and preventing disease. There might be times in your life where negative emotions may rise to the surface even after practicing gratitude. This may be a normal reaction to grief or loss, or a symptom of PTSD. Consulting your intuition could help you through this process. It may be necessary to seek professional guidance.

Health and Healing

Intuition and healing are closely linked. Both can help you evolve your consciousness. The two combined are the central fulcrum in my healing practice, and you will probably come to discover in your own life how this is true. The word "heal" means to make well again, to become free from injury or disease, to mend, or make sound or whole.[18]

Intuition will help you see the wholeness that already is you. You will learn to trust yourself. As you embark on a journey of discovering and listening to your intuition, you may increase your health and wellness. Personal and soul development naturally occur. You will be more receptive and better able to listen to your intuition. Being more healthy will strengthen receptivity, understanding, and implementation of your intuition. You will come to the truth of who you are and why you are here.

Intuition can help lower stress by helping you to have insight, guidance, and meaning around a particular situation happening in your life. It is estimated that 60 to 90 percent of doctor visits are in the mind-body, stress-related realm, and up to 33.7 percent of the population are affected by an anxiety disorder during their lifetime. Anxiety disorders are associated with enormous healthcare costs and a high burden of disease.[19,20] Anxiety may interfere with your ability to listen to your intuition and make good decisions, and it may affect your ability to carry out simple tasks.[21]

Conversely, your stress or anxiety may be trying to tell you something that is not working well in your life, grabbing your attention to listen to your intuition to help move you forward in positive ways. Your intuition can help you see stressful areas of your life from a fresh perspective that can heal your heart, mind, body, and spirit. Intuition can help you to make the best choices and come to understanding and acceptance about areas that may be difficult for you. You will then be able to come to the center of yourself and feel more peace, joy, and happiness that are correlated with better health outcomes.[22]

It's estimated that 75 percent of healthcare costs of chronic illness can be prevented by making healthy lifestyle choices.[23] Eighty percent of premature heart disease, stroke, and diabetes can be prevented.[24]

Listening to your intuition may help you choose to eat well, sleep, exercise, or move. Your enhanced intuitional knowledge can improve the quality of your relationships and direct the fun and healthy activities you choose to participate in. There's a better chance that if you engage in healthier choices you will stay more functionally independent longer in your life with less illness, disease, and suffering. (See health benefits listed on pages 59-60.)

The mind, body, spirit, and universe are inextricably linked—in fact from a transcendent perspective, they may be one and the same thing. But for the sake of easier understanding, I will refer to them separately, with the awareness that each so-called part can simultaneously influence the others, either positively or negatively. How well you feel connected to your spirit or energy may impact your mind, thoughts, emotions, beliefs, and the health of your body and energy levels. Thoughts, feelings, and emotions can affect the physical body and the spirit. How you take care of your physical body with rest, proper nutrition, and physical activity may impact your mind and spirit.

Woven throughout this book are ways that your intuition can help you heal, recover from an illness, and stay well. I would like to help you connect to healing tools that have the fundamental component of intuition. The activities involved may help you heal: feel whole, stay well, prevent disease, or possibly recover from an illness. Of course, there may be other ways or activities that you find beneficial, but these are the techniques I have used the most in my healing practice and for self-care. (Caveat: Be sure to find a qualified practitioner or consult with your primary healthcare practitioner before beginning any practice.)

> Health is being in harmony with the world view. Health is an intuitive perception of the universe and all its inhabitants as being of one fabric. Health is maintaining communication with the animals and plants and minerals and stars. It is knowing death and life and seeing no difference. It is blending and melding, seeking solitude and seeking companionship to understand one's many levels. Unlike the more "modern" notions, in shamanic society health is not the absence of feeling; no more so is it the absence of pain. Health is seeking out all of the experiences of Creation and turning them over and over, feeling their texture and multiple meanings. Health is expanding beyond one's singular state of consciousness to experience the ripples and waves of the universe.
>
> —Jeanne Achterberg[25]

Better Relationships

The more you feel gratitude, the more you will likely develop a stronger sense of compassion and intuition for yourself and others. This may allow you to see and understand with clarity and more easily connect with a state of love. Relationships can improve—with yourself and others. Improving relationships and improving compassion for the self and others may help you to be more present and calm in your interactions with others, enhance healthy boundaries, and facilitate healthy relationships.

Poets, philosophers, mystics, and spiritual leaders have been contemplating and sharing their thoughts about love for millennia. We are drawn to certain relationships to learn about love through them. There are many types of love, including friendship, family, romantic, universal, or spiritual love.[26] Universal love or *agape*, is the love for strangers, nature, or God. It encompasses the concept of altruism—unselfish concern for the welfare of others. Within all of these types of love relationships, we can learn how to give and receive unconditional love and self-love.

Through these relationships you have the opportunity to cultivate your love, intuition, and greater happiness. Love is the greatest healer. It can open the doorway for us to heal old wounds and to learn to love and accept ourselves. Through relationships we can learn how to love others and ourselves. This may be a relationship with people, a pet, animal, or higher power.

Within all relationships there is a sense of the self and the other. Martin Buber, a philosopher and scholar, in his book *I and Thou*, describes two types of relationships, the "I-It", and the "I-Thou." The I-It relationship is based on separateness from others where one uses another as an object. In contrast, in an I-Thou relationship, each person equally and completely turns toward the other with openness, ethical interactions, and total presence. Each participant is concerned for the other person. The honoring of the other is most important—not just their usefulness.[27, 28]

Buber shares that in the "I" toward "Thou," we move into existence in a relationship without bounds. He contends that human life finds its meaningfulness in relationships, and that all of our relationships will bring us ultimately into relationship with God—the Eternal Thou.

In countless yoga studios, students bow to each other and say, "Namaste." The I-Thou is what is kindly and lovingly being honored. They are essentially saying, "The light and love in me sees and honors the light and love in you." This is practiced when people in a Christian church shake each other's hands and say, "Peace be with you."

> *Your task is not to seek for love, but merely seek and find all*
> *the barriers within yourself that you have built against it.*
> —RUMI

Story

Sherry struggled with focus and attention. She had been diagnosed with attention deficit disorder by age eight. She was given medication that was designed to help her, but she felt it only made her thoughts seem more disorganized and negatively impacted her self-esteem. Despite her intuition telling her it was not helping her, she kept taking the medication because that's what the adults told her would help her. She continued to have difficulties in school, but she was able to graduate from high school.

When she turned eighteen, with the help of her physician, Sherry weaned herself off of the medication. She sought out the help of an occupational therapist because she wanted support reaching goals, such as gaining the confidence to take the steps to go to college. She discovered that much of her lack of focus and attention was probably due to low self-esteem as a result of verbal abuse from her mother. She was guided to listen to her intuition.

Sherry was able to begin healing her lack of self-worth, self-love, and self-esteem by being guided in relaxation techniques, meditation, guided imagery, and emotional freedom technique, also known as EFT or tapping. She gained greater confidence and connection to her intuition. She met her goals of going to college and began a relationship with a new partner. As her self-compassion increased, she was able to extend compassion to her mother, and her relationship with her mother improved.

Written Practice

- Why is intuition important to you?
- In what ways would you like your intuition to grow or guide you?

Experiential Practice:

Listen to Progressive Relaxation: http://www.youtube.com/watch?v=DNC5yhLIWFk&list=UUh_kFsasrtI2F5bEhn7402A

Progressive relaxation is a mind-body practice that relaxes the mind and body. We first begin with the breathwork, such as abdominal breathing, and then move to relaxing the whole body. It is a classic practice that has been time-tested and scientifically researched.

Sit or lie down in a comfortable position.

Diaphragm breathe—take a few slow, deep breaths in and out, letting your abdomen expand with each breath in and come back toward your body with each breath out.

Relax the body from head to feet, or from feet to head.

Bring your attention to your head, invite in relaxation, and allow it to come into the top of your head. Relaxation can be a feeling of warmth, or you can imagine a relaxing color coming into your body, while your body slowly becomes more heavy, calm, and still.

Allow the relaxation to come into your head, relaxing the muscles of your scalp on the top of your head, the sides, and back of your head.

Allow the relaxation to move through your forehead, around your eyes—letting all the muscles of your eyes relax, loosening your jaw, relaxing the muscles of your mouth and lips.

Let the base of your head and neck relax.

Loosen any tension in your throat. Let the relaxation move down your back from your upper back, to your middle back, and then to your lower back.

Allow the relaxation to spread across your shoulders and down your arms, to your upper arms, elbows, forearms, wrists, and hands.

Let the relaxation move across your chest, into your diaphragm and abdomen, allowing you to breathe easier.

The relaxation moves into your pelvis, loosening your hips, moving into your upper legs, knees, lower legs, ankles, and feet.

Notice how you feel. If there is any part of you that isn't as relaxed as you'd like, notice a place in your body where you do feel very relaxed, and let that feeling move into the area you would like to relax a little more.

Another version of progressive relaxation is to gently tense and release the various muscle groups of the body. Physically contract and hold the tension for a moment, and then slowly release and relax the muscle, for twice as long as it was contracted. This may physically help the muscles become more relaxed and is correlated with relaxing the mind.[29]

Journal:

- How was this experience for you?
- Was it easy or difficult to let your muscles relax?
- What areas of your body were more easy or difficult to relax?
- What else did you notice during this relaxation?

3. Where Does Intuition Come From?

If you want to know the secrets of the universe,
think in terms of energy, frequency, and vibration.
–Nikola Tesla

So where does intuition come from? That's similar to asking, "Where do thoughts, imagination, love, consciousness—or any of us—come from?" How do we receive this information? Is it inside of us or does it come from outside of us, or both?

It may be that it always exists, and we need to learn to gently uncover it or allow it to come forward. "Just be," many wise sages have said for eons. Intuition may have always been there, just waiting for us to quiet our minds so we can listen and feel what it may be wanting to share with us. Perhaps, because we don't know where it comes from or how to recognize it, we inhibit our ability to listen to it.

Theories exist about where this unique way of knowing—intuition—comes from. Here are a few ways it may come into our awareness.

Everything Is Energy

Intuition is a form of energy. Quantum physics, also known as quantum mechanics, tells us that everything is energy, including matter.

Quantum physics is the study of matter and energy at its most basic level. Within an atom, energy comes in the form of indivisible packets called quanta that behave likes waves, and waves behave like particles.[1]

But what is energy? There are several definitions:[2]

1. Ability to be active: the physical or mental strength that allows you to do things. *They devoted all their energy to the completion of the project.*
2. Natural enthusiasm and effort. *She puts a lot of energy into her work.*
3. Usable power that comes from heat, electricity, etc. *The newer appliances conserve more energy.*
4. The ability of something (such as heat, light, or running water) to be active or do work. *Kinetic energy and particles with high kinetic energies.*
5. A type of power that some people believe a person or place produces. *There's good/positive energy in this room.*

Albert Einstein showed us that $E = mc^2$; that is, "Energy equals mass times the speed of light squared." This equation essentially means that energy and mass (matter) are interchangeable; they are different forms of the same thing. Given the right conditions, energy can become mass, and mass can become energy.[3]

Therefore, when we look closely at who we really are, we will find that we are beings of energy and vibration who radiate a specific frequency or light. Inside the atom is a small invisible tornado-like vortex, with small energy vortices called quarks and photons that make up the structure of the atom. There is no physical structure to the atom or what we recognize as physical objects. Atoms seem to be made of invisible energy. Tangible matter does not exist.[4] Expanding this understanding beyond Newtonian physics to include the universe, we see that it is a holistic entanglement of immaterial energy waves and more than merely a collection of physical parts.[5]

Energy may be described as life force, frequency, or light that is also known as *qi* (pronounced "chee") or *prana*. It is the vital force in the cosmos and in and around our bodies that gives and maintains life. Some may refer to it as our spirit, soul, or universal life energy. Our energy can impact us in all areas of our life. Energy is a virtual blueprint and foundation of our being; the physical, mental, emotional, and spiritual aspects. When it is flowing properly, we feel at our best. When it is constricted, limited, or blocked, we may not feel that we're operating as well.[6] Even if we're not completely consciously aware of it, we emanate energy and can sense it all around us in all of its various forms: a house, tree, dog, street, food, people, emotions, feelings, sentiments, sound, etc. (Learn how to cultivate your energy in Chapter 7.)

Everything Is Connected

Quantum entanglement or *nonlocality theory* teaches us that everything is connected, and we may have knowledge of each other's state no matter the distance. Einstein, along with physicists Boris Podolsky and Nathan Rosen, discovered quantum entanglement.[7] It was first explained in the "EPR papers"—Einstein, Podolsky, and Rosen—in 1935, and at times is referred to as the *EPR paradox*. The papers describe that when objects are apart from each other, potentially by enormous distances—even billions of light years, they can instantaneously know each other's state. This is a giant leap faster than Einstein's speed of light, which was thought to be the maximum speed for everything in the universe. So, according to quantum entanglement theory, given the right conditions, information can be transferred instantaneously.[8]

Experiments have shown that once particles have interacted, they will remain connected and entangled. They will continue to affect each other, regardless of how far they are separated by physical distance. Einstein called this "spooky action at a distance" and had a difficult time accepting what he was observing. Research has continued to support this theory to this day, and physics is still discovering new ways to explain and understand the universe.[9]

Intuition is a sudden knowing of information. If everything is connected (for instance, we have an established connection to a source because our particles have already interacted), and we have the potential to access information in a nonlinear and nonlocal way, it (knowing) may occur quickly. This may explain why an intuitive experience is often described as having "a sudden flash of insight." There are waves, particles, and photons of light immediately entering into awareness.

The Brain

A commonly accepted Western European understanding about consciousness, thought, or perception is that they come from the brain, and that all motor and sensory functions come from specific regions that can be correlated to maps in the brain. Therefore, with this theory, intuition resides in or comes from the brain. There is evidence to support this neurological understanding.[10] However, research continues to evolve in the quest for understanding consciousness, perception, and awareness. Consciousness may extend or reside beyond the physical body—which is the common understanding in most of the world's indigenous and traditional wisdom cultures.

Many researchers have described intuition as coming from the right side of the brain in the outdated "right brain-left brain theory." This popular, but not entirely accurate, theory stated that there is a difference between what the right and the left side of the brain control. Neuropsychologist and neurobiologist Roger Sperry conducted split-brain experiments and won a Nobel Prize in 1981 for his research to reduce or eliminate seizures by cutting the corpus callosum (brain tissue that connects the two hemispheres of the brain). While studying the effects of epilepsy, he found that the left and right hemispheres are specialized in different tasks.[11]

The right half of the brain was thought to be responsible for intuition, creativity, being thoughtful, expressing emotions, images, music, and subjectivity, while the left side of the brain was more adept with logic, analytical thinking, and language.[12] This theory is often believed because we may experience having two sides to us—the loving and empathic side, and the analytical and judging side. The physical, mental, and emotional consequences of neurological conditions, such as a stroke or brain injury affecting certain areas of the brain, may have coincided with these regions of the brain. There is continued exploration and debate about how the brain functions as a whole unit or through separate parts.[13]

Your intuition may help your brain change and develop in positive ways. The brain may be more plastic or changeable than has been previously thought. For hundreds of years, science has believed that the brain's anatomy or structure—thus function, behavior, and consciousness—were static, "hardwired," and could not change. It was thought that brain cells were unable to be replaced and would only change during the decline from aging, from injury, or death. We now understand that the brain can change itself through activity and thought and has the potential to behave in a more holistic way through neuroplasticity. *Neuro* comes from "neuron" or nerve cells in the brain and nervous system, and *plastic* means changeable, malleable, or modifiable.[14]

Another theory about where intuition may come from focuses on the brain's pineal gland, known as "the third eye," considered for millennia by Eastern spiritual traditions to be the inner eye or inner sight or the all-knowing, all-seeing eye. This is also called the sixth *chakra*—where the mind's eye, intuition, and wisdom are thought to be located. This can be seen in many ancient healing traditions, such as Traditional Chinese Medicine (TCM) that practices energy healing, acupuncture, acupressure, and herbal medicine. "Chakra" is from the Sanskrit language meaning "spinning wheel of light," where energy is believed to enter into and go out of the body. Many people meditate upon the sixth as well as other chakras. Although science has yet to confirm the existence of chakras, science has shown that when people meditate and intentionally balance their perceived energy centers, it may positively affect the central nervous system.

The pineal gland fascinated René Descartes, a French philosopher and mathematician. He regarded it as the "principal seat of the soul, and the place in which all our thoughts are formed."[15] A seeker of truth, Descartes famously offered the meditation for us all to consider about our existence, "I think, therefore I am."[16]

Intuition and consciousness may be difficult to quantify and relegate to one part of the body. Even neuroscientists debate where consciousness resides—inside or outside of the brain.[17] Filter theory suggests that the brain is a conduit for consciousness to flow into and out of versus being the creator of it. Accordingly, the physical brain may act as a filter, or reducing valve, of human perception that connects to a larger universal consciousness or the "collective mind."[18] Our consciousness may actually live in an energy field surrounding the brain in another dimension, and the whole body may be a conduit that collaborates with consciousness. The brain may exchange information with the cosmos.[19] This ability is described in *One Mind: How Our Individual Mind is Part of a Greater Consciousness and Why it Matters* by Larry Dossey, MD. Dr. Dossey is pioneer in integrative healthcare who merges spirit and medicine.

The Heart

Intuition may come from the heart. Throughout history, ancient societies, philosophers, poets, and prophets have regarded the heart as the source of love, wisdom, intuition, the soul, and positive emotions. The Egyptians believed that the heart was connected to spiritual dimensions. After death, the heart was weighed to see how much good and evil it contained, and it was put in special urns for burial, and the brain was discarded. Thus, there is a disparity between what ancient traditions believed and modern predominant science's teaching that the heart solely provides a physical function.[20]

Images of the heart can be seen in religious iconography and are elevated, imploring us to contemplate what it represents: the highest values. Most spiritual or religious practices teach the importance of the heart and being loving and kind to the self and others. Adages such as "listen to your heart," "follow your heart," or "lead from the heart" must derive from a physical feeling of well-being in the body when we take direction from that organ or its location in the chest. The positive effect of doing so is likely why these sayings have survived so long. As we connect with our heart center, we shift into a loving, compassionate awareness. From this neutral, nonjudgmental place we may switch into our intuitive awareness. When we are more coherent—not emotional, thinking, confused, etc.—we are able to listen to our heart more clearly.

> For thousands of years, the human heart was viewed as the center of thought, emotion, memory, and personality—the master organ of the body. Traditions to honor the role of the heart were created and passed down generation after generation. Ceremonies were performed. And techniques were developed to utilize the heart's function as a conduit of intuition and healing. . . . Growing evidence suggests that heart and the brain work together to share the role of the body's master organs—two separate organs connected through a common network of information.
>
> – GREGG BRADEN, RESILIENCE FROM THE HEART[21]

Being connected to your heart and consistently practicing being in this loving state can assist greatly with intuition, wellness, and healing. When I was beginning my meditation practice, a teacher led me to focus on the heart in meditation. I imagined entering into my heart to cultivate a higher loving state of being, and to strongly sense this loving vibration of light. I then visualized the light of my heart connecting with the center of my brain (the third eye). In this state, I could more effortlessly listen to intuitive and wise messages.

There is research that supports what the ancients intuitively understood. The HeartMath Institute is an internationally recognized non-profit research and education organization dedicated to helping people reduce stress, self-regulate emotions, and build energy and resilience for healthier, happier lives. It has conducted research on the heart and brain coherence, concluding that we register information in our heart before it is received by the brain. HeartMath Institute highlights that the heart informs the brain more than the other way around, and the two work simultaneously together:

> Most of us have been taught in school that the heart is constantly responding to 'orders' sent by the brain in the form of neural signals. However, it is not as commonly known that the heart actually sends more signals to the brain than the brain sends to the heart! Moreover, these heart signals have a significant effect on brain function—influencing

emotional processing as well as higher cognitive faculties, such as attention, perception, memory, and problem-solving. In other words, not only does the heart respond to the brain, but the brain continuously responds to the heart.

–THE HEART-BRAIN CONNECTION. THE SCIENCE BEHIND
THE emWAVE® AND INNER BALANCE™ TECHNOLOGIES.[22]

Rollin McCraty, PhD, the vice president and director of research at the HeartMath Institute, says, "The heart is a sensory organ and acts as a sophisticated information-encoding and processing center that enables it to learn, remember, and make independent functional decisions."[23] He adds that the heart and the brain generate an electromagnetic field. McCraty explains, "The heart generates the largest electromagnetic field in the body. The electrical field as measured in an electrocardiogram (ECG) is about sixty times greater in amplitude than the brain waves recorded in an electroencephalogram (EEG)."[24]

The "Little Brain" in the Heart

In 1991, J. Andrew Armour, MD, PhD, of the University of Montreal, found about 40,000 specialized neurons, called *sensory neurites*, in the heart. This network of communication is known as the "little brain" in the heart.[25] McCraty stated, "The *heart-brain*, as it is commonly called, or intrinsic cardiac nervous system, is an intricate network of complex ganglia, neurotransmitters, proteins, and support cells, the same as those of the brain in the head. The heart-brain's neural circuitry enables it to act independently of the cranial brain to learn, remember, make decisions, and even feel and sense."[26] The neurites in the heart provide many similar functions found in the brain. Dr. Armour said, "It has become clear in recent years that a sophisticated, two-way communication occurs between the heart and the brain, with each influencing the other's function."[27]

The heart's little brain functions in two separate and associated ways. It can function: (1) *independently of* the cranial brain to think, learn, remember, and even sense our inner and outer worlds on its own; and (2) *in harmony with* the cranial brain to give us the benefit of a single, potent neural network shared by the two separate organs.

These functions include:

- Providing the heart-based wisdom known as "heart intelligence"
- Promoting intentional states of deep intuition
- Allowing for intentional precognitive abilities
- Directing the heart's communication with sensory neurites in other organs in the body[28]

Love

One of the quickest and easiest ways to connect with your intuition is to focus on your heart and connect with a state of love. When you are in this loving state, you are in a higher-consciousness state, often called "your higher self," which helps you to see and act from an intuitive perspective.

Focus on your heart. As you connect with your heart center, you shift into a loving, compassionate awareness. From this neutral, nonjudgmental place you may more easily switch into intuitive consciousness. When we are in this more coherent state—less emotional, less confused, and more neutral—we are able to listen to intuition more clearly.

You can do this by placing your hand on your heart, or focus your attention there, and say, "I am loving presence," or "I am loving awareness," as the spiritual leader Ram Dass suggests. Focusing on what you are grateful for or who or what you love can help you reach this state. Practicing meditation regularly will help you access it more easily.

According to McCraty, there are electromagnetic signals produced by your heart that can be registered in the brains of people who are around you. Even when you're not consciously communicating with them, your physiological responses can sync up with your mate's during times of empathetic interactions.[23]

Heart rate variability has been correlated with health and fitness. It is the amount of variability your heart has in between your heartbeats. It is a marker of physiological resilience and behavioral flexibility—how well your mind and body can handle stressors and environmental demands.[22]

The more relaxed and positive you feel, the more heart rate variability you will have, and the more your heart and brain will function in a coherent state. When you're functioning from an intuitive state—that is, a relaxed and positive state—there is likely more heart rate variability. Therefore, the more you abide in these states of consciousness, the better you will feel, with a stronger ability to cope with and respond to what may come your way in life, and the more healthy you will be.

Heart Wave Coherence

The HeartMath Institute has created simple steps to achieve what they term a "coherent state" or "coherence." The power of your heart can help balance thoughts and emotions. This is when there is more heart rate variability allowing you to feel better and have more mental clarity. This can be achieved in about one minute. Connecting with the heart and feeling more positive echoes the compassion, mindfulness, and lovingkindness meditations. The more that we are in a coherent state, the more easily we can listen to the higher intelligence of intuition.

> Using the power of your heart to balance thoughts and emotions, you can achieve energy, mental clarity, and feel better fast anywhere. Use Quick Coherence especially when you begin feeling a draining emotion, such as frustration, irritation, anxiety, or anger. Find a feeling of ease and inner harmony that's reflected in more balanced heart rhythms, facilitating brain function and more access to higher intelligence.
>
> -THE HEARTMATH INSTITUTE

Quick Coherence® Technique

1. Focus your attention in the area of the heart. Imagine your breath is flowing in and out of your heart or chest area, breathing a little slower and deeper than usual. Find an easy rhythm that's comfortable.
2. As you continue heart-focused breathing, make a sincere attempt to experience a regenerative feeling such as appreciation or care for someone or something in your life.

Quick Steps

1. Heart-Focused Breathing
2. Activate a positive or a renewing feeling[29]

Permission for use by HeartMath®

Spirituality

Perhaps intuition is our spiritual self, the soul, or maybe it comes from our connection with the "All" or spiritual sources, such as God, Creator, higher power, angels, guides, the soul, or nature—however you conceive of that. Spirituality and quantum physics may not be that far apart from each other. Perhaps they are simply different languages for the same phenomena.

Throughout time, prophets, mystics, saints, sages, yogis, wise beings, and shamanic healers have received intuitive messages. Most spiritual or religious practices are based around this central tenet—communication with a divine source or being(s). It is thought that when one is in prayer, contemplation, or meditation, communication is occurring with a God(s) or divine source.

Your personal connection to and exploration of spirituality is unique to you. Connecting with your intuition regularly may help develop or strengthen your spirituality. In my personal experiences, it wasn't until I began developing my intuition that I was able to develop a personal relationship with my spirituality. (Read more about spirituality and intuition in Chapter 11.)

Consciousness and intuition have been researched, explored, and shared deeply by parapsychologist Jeffrey Mishlove, PhD. As the host of New Thinking Allowed on YouTube, he has been interviewing thought leaders on these topics since the 1980s—first on the *Thinking Allowed* public television series. His several books include: *The Roots of Consciousness—The Classic Encyclopedia of Consciousness Studies, Revised and Expanded*; *Psi Development Systems*; and *The PK Man*. He is also the former president of the Intuition Network. Through his dedication and body of work, he will encourage you to cultivate and apply your intuitive abilities.[30]

Listen to the interview: "The Intuitive Mind," with Jeffrey Mishlove and Emmy Vadnais: https://youtu.be/O0OprloE7B8

True Self

What is your true self? It may be a deep connection to the part of you that is beyond judgments, thoughts, worry, perceptions, beliefs, projections, and dualism. When you move beyond or expand out of small thoughts, you may experience being fully and completely yourself.

Awareness of this part of ourselves may come from being in a loving and relaxed state. As our minds become more quiet and free from negative thoughts, worries, concerns, or emotions, the more aware we can be. We are then able to listen, receive, and be with this wise part of ourselves. This is one of the reasons meditation has become more popular. People want to experience this state, and it is achievable.

Wherever true self may come from, experiment with which ways work best for you to get in touch with it. It may be a combination of all of these.

Written Exercise

- Where do you believe intuition comes from?
- Is it something we're all born with, a learned ability, or both?

- Do you believe intuition comes from within us, outside of us, or both?
- How do you define "spirituality"?
- Do you believe intuition is related to spirituality? If yes, how? If not, how are they different?

Experiential Practice

Think of something that you would like more insight into or clarity about. Write it down. Take note of your emotions, feelings, and thoughts. Listen to the Open Heart Meditation or practice one of the other meditations in this book. Then, think about the situation and feel into it with all of your senses. How do you see or feel it differently? What new insights have come forward? Journal your experience.

Listen to the Open Heart Meditation: https://youtu.be/T6mB-fxvGsbY

Allow yourself to get into a comfortable position.

Take a few slow, gentle, deep breaths in and out. Allow your abdomen to expand with each breath in, hold it for a moment, then exhale slowly. And again, gentle breath in, hold, then exhale slowly. Continue breathing gently and effortlessly. . . .

Find the Light in Heart, spread that light out through your whole being and body, letting it expand past your physical body about a foot (or more). Visualize the light permeating through your whole being, every tissue, every joint, every cell. . . .

Feel this light. You are this light. . . .

Allow yourself to connect with Gratitude, a feeling of gratefulness and thankfulness. . . .

Focus your attention on what you are grateful for. You may wish to give thanks. . . .

Allow the feeling of gratitude to expand through your whole being and body. . . .

Allow yourself to connect with Love; *you may think of someone or something you love. You may wish to say, "I love you."*

Allow the feeling of love to expand through your whole being and body.

Allow yourself to connect with Joy, a feeling of levity and happiness.

Think of something or someone that gives you joy; a smile may come across your face. . . .

Allow the feeling of joy to expand through your whole being and body. . . .

Allow yourself to connect with Compassion, being able to feel and understand another's pain, sorrow, suffering, or joy. You may even feel compassion for yourself. . . .

You may wish to say, "I feel you and I understand."

Spread Light their way. . . .

Allow the feeling of compassion to expand through your whole being and body. . . .

Spend as much time with gratitude, love, joy, and compassion as you wish. . . .

Feel the radiance of your heart being open.

4. How You May Perceive Intuition

Logic will get you from A to B.
Imagination will take you everywhere.
–Albert Einstein

WE ALL HAVE INTUITIVE ABILITIES, and we each have a unique way of perceiving intuition. Knowing the natural ways that you intuit will build your confidence and trust when you are listening to intuition's wisdom. Once you have an idea of what senses are most often engaged when listening to your intuition, you will be better able to recognize it. Then, you can strengthen these senses and learn to increase your ability with additional senses.

Between the ages of three and seven, people are generally the most connected to their intuition and imagination, and they use fantasy play as well as symbolic thought and language to communicate. Do you recall having any imaginary friends when you were very young? Were you encouraged to have your friend or do you recall being told it wasn't real? After age four, through socialization, development, and conditioning, logical thinking begins to replace *intuitive thought*—a term described by developmental psychologist Jean Piaget.[1] If a child is raised in an environment where their intuitive abilities are encouraged and accepted, then they will likely retain more of this ability throughout their life. If they are raised in an environment where they are taught it's not real or okay to talk about it, then they will likely suppress this ability.[2] But it is never too late to learn to bring this ability forward.

Senses

All or some of your senses may be utilized when receiving intuitive impressions: vision, hearing, taste, smell, touch, emotions, and/or feelings or a felt sense in the body known as *interoception*. You may also experience intuition as images in your mind's eye, symbols, flashes of insight, or dream events. Just like everything else, intuition is a form of energy or frequency that you can perceive from within or outside of yourself. To enhance your intuition, it can be helpful to draw upon physical cues in the environment, such as how something looks or sounds, a person's body language, or their facial expressions—along with your intuition. It's best to take all of your senses into account as best you can and discern what may be the most accurate intuitive impression.

Words have been used to describe intuiting with each sense. *Clair* is a French word that means "clear," as in being able to see clearly. Clair combined with each sense has been used to describe intuitive abilities.

- Clairvoyance—"clear vision." You may see things in the physical world, or you may see in your mind with "inner-sight" or "insight" images while you are dreaming, either awake or when you are asleep.
- Clairaudience—"clear hearing." You may hear as if it is real, or you may hear in your mind. It may be like talking to yourself, but different than your own thoughts.
- Clairgustance—"clear tasting." You may experience a taste in your mouth that is providing you intuitive information.
- Clairalience—"clear smelling." You may experience smells that indicate an intuitive message coming forward.
- Clairsentience—"clear feeling." That may be experienced as physical sensations in your body, feelings, or emotions, or a deep knowing or "inner knowing," such as experiencing

tingling, heaviness, discomfort, pain, being uplifted, or joy in any part of your body. This may include being empathic: being able to feel how another person or animal feels, using all of the senses including interoception.

Emotions

We all experience various emotions throughout the day. Emotions can inform you, guide you, protect you, and can help connect you to yourself, others, and the world. When listening to your intuition, emotions can help you receive information around a particular situation or topic. However, it's necessary to discern which emotions are informing you to give you true intuitive impressions and which ones come from your conditioned thoughts, beliefs, or are wounded parts of you that may need healing.

Emotions may help you to have an accurate intuitive assessment by feeling a reaction to something that may indicate that it is positive, neutral, or not so good. To do this well, it's important to move past pain, wounds, conditioned thoughts, beliefs, judgments, emotions, feelings, wishes, or desires. You will then be better able to trust what are true intuitive emotions or gut reactions that are accurate assessments of situations. Practicing the exercises in this book will help you with this.

It is necessary to regularly engage in activities that relax and clear your mind and body. Doing so will help you to be in a neutral state where it is easiest to discern what is real intuition and what are your personal feelings or projection of emotions, negative reactions, wishes, desires, outcomes, beliefs, or judgments. Equally important is to discern what is your intuition versus what you may be picking up from someone else's emotions. And at times, feeling others' emotions and interoception may help you with your intuition and in relationships. You can simply ask inside yourself, "Is this mine or someone else's?" Listen and feel the response. With practice and feedback, you will have more clarity and trust what is yours.

Candace Pert, PhD, author of *Molecules of Emotion*, states that the body is the subconscious of the mind. By paying attention to your emotions and body, you can more fully access your mind and support your overall soul and personal development and health. Your body and emotions will help bring aspects from the subconscious into the conscious. Many healthcare practitioners believe that wellness or disease and disharmony begin with the state of the mind, thoughts, emotions, or consciousness, which then affects the body.

If you are providing care or support to someone else with your intuition, it can be particularly helpful to use your intuitive senses to understand how someone is feeling. You can become more compassionate toward them and understand why they may make certain choices and behave the way they do. Your intuition can bring focus to an area that may be wounded or hurt that needs attention, care, love, or healing.

Emotion defined: the affective aspect of consciousness, a state of feeling, a conscious mental reaction (such as anger or fear) subjectively experienced as strong feeling usually directed toward a specific object and typically accompanied by physiological and behavioral changes in the body.

Etymology: Middle French, from *emouvoir* to stir up, from Old French *esmovoir*, from Latin *emovēre* to remove, displace, from *e-* + *movēre* to move.

First known use: 1579.[3]

Intuition can help you to find the symbolic light in the dark. It can help you dive past emotions, feelings, thoughts, and beliefs that may be limiting you or are making you unwell; intuition can transform them to positive states. It can assist you with grief, loss, or coping during times of change or transition. Intuition can assist you to be less likely to misperceive situations, internally and externally. It can help you to be more resilient. With fewer attachments and less pain from the past to react to, you are apt to see more clearly.

As you uncover your light within, the layers obscuring your intuition will likely transform and heal. These parts of you will become more apparent and have information to tell you. As you quiet yourself and go within, you may learn about parts of you that have felt ignored, alone, or isolated. You may encounter unresolved pain or grief that will require and receive attention in ways it hasn't before. This may rewire neurological connections to new and more positive stories in your life, with lowered cortisol or stress hormone levels.

Some say, all there is, is love and fear. If you are empathic, you may experience other people's feelings. It is important to discern and understand which emotions are your own and which belong to others. As you move toward more awareness, you will also begin to see when you are projecting your subconscious emotions onto others and when you may blame them for your feelings. You need to pay attention and discern what you are feeling and where it is coming from.

It may be helpful to heal past emotions that are based on past wounds or experiences that cause biases. Once healed and cleared, the emotions you experience in an intuitive state of consciousness will inform you more accurately. We need to be positive and also release unwanted negative beliefs, emotions, and feelings about past situations.

Several techniques that may help to transform negative feeling states into positive ones have well-researched health benefits. The approaches listed in this section may assist you. Mindfulness and Emotional Freedom Technique (EFT) are two approaches that can help directly transform limiting emotions, thoughts, and beliefs. Regularly listening to your intuition will help you to make sense of past situations to heal them and make good choices going forward.

Emotional Boundaries

Practice being in a neutral state. From there you will be better able to more cleanly and clearly connect with another. We can "push each other's buttons" and get enmeshed through judgments, expectations, beliefs, transference, countertransference, etc. This can be an opportunity for healing.

If you are sensing something from someone, you may ask yourself:
What's mine, what's theirs?
Am I to do anything with this information?

Hold the intention:

Only good from me, only good to me.
Only good from them, only good to them.
They have all of them, I have all of me.

You can imagine that you are "beaming" them or sending them love, light, and compassion. This may seem challenging, especially if you feel upset with someone, but this may be exactly what this relationship dynamic needs to neutralize or make the energy more positive.

Empaths

Empaths experience *empathy*. They are able to sense what someone else may be experiencing. Through clairsentience—emotions, feelings, interoception, energy, or all of their senses—empaths are able to rely on their intuition. Empaths are highly sensitive to all sorts of perceptions and cues. They seem to be correlated with the "intuition-feeling" personality types according to the Myers-Briggs Personality Type Indicator, and they can be described by this term.[4]

I believe most of us are able to intuit empathically. Many people experience this trait and do not realize they are sensing emotions and feelings from other people, animals, or living things and have learned or been conditioned to dismiss this. They live day to day, not knowing why they feel or think the way they do. Thinking everything is their own experience, they may actually be picking up others' experiences or the energy around them. We are all able to intuitively perceive information about a person, place, or object, and when we concentrate and focus on a specific topic, sometimes such information flows into us unbeknownst to us.

The Myers-Briggs Personality Type Indicator describes four basic personality types: Extrovert-Introvert, Sensing-Intuition, Thinking-Feeling, and Perceiving-Judging. People who have intuition-feeling, or "NF" types, have an interest in mysticism, the occult, meditation, psi research, and esoteric practices. The opposite of this type is the sensing-thinking or "ST" types who seem to have no interest in these topics and are more focused on materialistic, rational, and logical ideas. Dean Radin, PhD, chief scientist at the Institute of Noetic Sciences, states that there is a bias toward the materialistic and pragmatic interests among people who control funding and power in large organizations. Conversely, a lack of people who are interested in mystical and intuitive phenomena exists.

"Not surprisingly, sensing-thinking people tend to be focused on the here and now, the materialistic, and rational, logical ideas. Sensing-thinking-judging (STJ) types are interested in management, leadership, and authority in hierarchical organizations, and in the use of power to control rather than in creative or novel ideas. The extroverted STJ person is most prominent in Western culture. When the Myers-Briggs Type [Indicator] was given to thousands of people in large organizations, 60 percent of the top executive positions had STJ personalities, and the proportion of STJ types increased as their management level increased. Only about 1 percent of the top executives had the opposite, intuitive-feeling-perceiving or NFP, personalities."[5]

Is it possible that how people perceive their experiences is really a "top-down" learning process from those who seem to hold the most power or leadership positions? Is it possible that we can all learn new ways of perceiving through intuition? I absolutely believe it to be so.

Story

After quitting a job she hated, Barbara had been in employment free-fall for three years. She was nearing fifty and nobody would hire her. One day she received a flyer for a workshop, and as she opened it, she felt as though the paper exploded and pulsed. Without questioning it, she called the number given for registration. When she heard the name of the company, again there was a sense of explosion that made chills go up and down her spine.

The subject of the workshop was not something that she had been seeking, but she went. It was interesting to her, but not earthshaking. But feeling as if she was still hearing the explosion of the name of the company, she decided to seek out their product: a magazine. She bought a copy, read it with some difficulty as it was way more esoteric than what she was attracted to, but still whatever had happened with the explosion of the name of the company reverberated inside her. So she asked the man in charge of the company if he needed any help and she sent a resume.

She was hired part-time. It turned out that there were things at this company—other forms of communication besides the esoteric magazine—that mesmerized her. And this part-time job proved to be the first step into a career that she loves.

Had she allowed herself to be stopped by the things that had put her off, she would have missed the opening. But instead she trusted her sense of explosion and pulsating of the flyer and the company name.

Messages

Intuition may be clear, direct guidance. You may hear words or see pictures or images in your mind's eye, such as when you receive messages during meditation or contemplative prayer—or it can happen when you are simply going about your day. At times, when there is something that you need to pay attention to or that your consciousness is ready to hear, it will repeat itself to you. For example, you may hear the same message from three different sources in one day: while listening to a song in the morning, in conversation with someone midday, or on a billboard later in the day on your drive home from work.

Symbols

Intuition may come in the form of symbols or images. Before we learned to talk, read, or write, we thought in pictures and relied on our senses and imagination to experience and interact with the world.[6] Symbols, by definition, often need to be interpreted.

Symbol defined: something that stands for, represents, or suggests another thing, esp. an object used to represent something abstract; emblem: *the dove is a symbol for Peace.*[7]

Symbols help us interpret inner and outer worlds. Symbols can come to us from any of our five senses: what we may see, hear, taste, smell, or feel. Their meanings remain flexible even though they may have universal significance. Symbols need to be interpreted in context to their situation to understand what they are telling us.

Trust your own interpretations. This is your intuition speaking to you. Use discernment and feel within. There are books and references to help you interpret meanings that can be helpful. However, if you want to strengthen your intuition, begin with your own interpretation before looking up a symbol.

Dreams

Your intuition may come to you in the form of messages or clues to aspects of your life or relationships while you are dreaming. A dream feeling or image may stay with you throughout the day; perhaps it wants more exploration and understanding. Dreams may provide direct messages or they may need to be interpreted symbolically to understand what they are telling you.

You may perceive intuition while you are awake—during daydreaming. Sometimes staring out a window can provide respite from over-thinking and relax the mind and help you to receive intuition more effortlessly. Have you ever been working on something or thinking about a problem you were trying hard to solve and you took a break and went on a walk or allowed your mind to drift? And suddenly you started to see it all more clearly and found a way forward? This is often a helpful way to allow your intuition to speak to you.

How Will I Know It's My Intuition?

Being able to discern when you have an accurate intuitive impression is its own art form. Do you remember learning how to ride a bike? Do you recall when you were first trying to get your balance and felt a bit wobbly or maybe even fell down? Do you recall when you finally caught your balance and you were just flying down the path, not even thinking about your balance, and how good that felt? Intuition is like that. When you're in an intuitive state of consciousness, you're not really working at it or wondering if it's your intuition, because it is just happening and you will have a feeling of being in the flow (or zone) with it. I also liken it to being dialed in to a radio station. Do you recall hearing static and garbled noises until you were on the precise point of the station? That is how it feels when you are connected to your intuition. You will know when you are dialed in to the right frequency because the static of your mind and wondering if it's accurate disappears.

Here are some ways that will help you know it's your intuition speaking to you:

- Know which senses are generally most active for you with intuition. A simple way to identify them is to notice what senses are engaged during the Special Place Guided Imagery[8] (see page 87) or any other guided imagery where all of the senses are active in your experience. There are usually one to three dominant senses that will be easier for you to engage in. As you continue to cultivate your intuition, it is likely that these senses will become stronger and more clear. Over time, other senses may become stronger.

- Hindsight is one of the best ways to know if you were accurate with intuition. Think of a situation where you've said to yourself: "I should have known better," and over time that has proved to be correct; or "Something just felt right," and over time it was clear that you had made the right choice. Then pay attention to *how* you knew. What was it that made you know at that time? Was there a time that you wished you had listened to your "gut" but ignored it? What was a clue that you dismissed? In the future, you can learn to pay more attention to these parts of you and allow them to guide you.

- Trusting what you are receiving will help you perceive your intuition! If you doubt it, you will block it. Whether you are sure or not that what you are receiving is accurate, be open, let it all come into your awareness and sift through all of the information. Try the suggestions and exercises in this book. In time your intuition will become clearer; over time you will just know.

Writing Reflection

- What senses are most active for you with your intuition?
- As a child, were you raised in an environment where your intuitive abilities were encouraged and accepted, or were you taught it's not real or okay to talk about?
- When do you recall knowing your intuition was speaking to you?
- How do you know it was your intuition—what senses were most active?
- Is it possible that fewer people are exposed to valuing intuition because of a bias and preference toward materialism in Western culture?
- Is it possible that as more people learn how to connect and develop their intuition, there will be more people aware of their innate abilities who are supported to develop their Intuition-Feeling type?
- If more people were connected to their intuition, how do you think or feel this would impact each individual, our society, culture, the world, environment, and all of its inhabitants?

5. Ways to Connect with Intuition

Do you have the patience to wait
till your mud settles and the water is clear?
Can you remain unmoving
till the right action arises by itself?
—Lao Tzu, from *Tao Te Ching*

BEING CONNECTED TO YOUR INTUITION is like letting the mud settle from the water in your mind until it is clear. There are several ways to help the mud settle, for you to connect with your intuition more easily. Any activity that puts you in the *relaxation response* state can connect you to your intuition.

Your logical thinking, desires, judgments, emotions, conditioning, and emotional attachments—the mud in the water—can keep you from listening to and connecting with your intuition. Instead, from your neutral, nonjudgmental, compassionate, and loving core, you can observe your inner and outer worlds and be more open to receive clear insight and guidance.

There are several ways discussed throughout this book that suggest how you can connect with your intuition, including exercises at the end of each chapter. You can begin connecting to your intuition for thirty seconds by simply holding a meaningful object—such as stone, a picture, or some type of talisman—or saying a quick affirmation, meditation, or prayer. Activities can be broken down by thirty seconds, three to five minutes, and up to twenty to thirty minutes or more. It's okay to be where you are at any point in your journey. Be gentle with yourself, and even at times laugh at yourself as this beautiful process unfolds.

The following methods may help you, or you may find your own unique way that is enjoyable to help the mud settle. Discover what will work best for you, such as:

- Paying attention to all of your senses
- Relaxation techniques
- Meditation
- Guided imagery/hypnosis
- Prayer or connection to your higher power
- Ritual, or space clearing
- Divinatory tools such as tarot, *I Ching*, or runes
- Yoga
- T'ai chi
- Creative activity
- Journaling, drawing, painting, or making collage
- Play
- Spending time in nature
- Dreaming
- Listening to music or sounds
- Toning or singing
- Dancing
- Going for a walk
- Physical exercise
- Gardening
- Cooking
- Massage therapy, reflexology, acupressure, acupuncture, craniosacral therapy, or any other relaxing healing modality
- Taking a bath or shower
- Any activity or "non-doing" that gets you out of streaming everyday thoughts and into the present moment; i.e., not thinking of the past or future—just being

The Relaxation Response and Meditation

While there are several types of meditation, the common feature seems to be that they all can induce the relaxation response, coined by Herbert Benson, MD. Director emeritus of the Benson-Henry Institute (BHI) at Massachusetts General Hospital, Benson also is professor of medicine at Harvard Medical School and author or co-author of more than 190 scientific publications and twelve books. His body of work demonstrates scientific research on the mind-body connection and the power of the mind in healing.

There is so much emphasis on "doing" in our culture that we can unwittingly reach unhealthy levels. We do need a certain amount of movement, energy, stress, or tension to move us forward in our lives. Stress can enhance performance to a point, but when a line is crossed, excessive stress impedes performance and can cause or exacerbate illness or disease. Fear, worry, anxiety, negative thought patterns, racing heart, high blood pressure, anger, greater vulnerability to pain, as well as poor sleep, eating habits, and lifestyle choices can all be exacerbated by stress. Relaxation can help us to "rest and digest" and is the antidote for the *stress response* that can cause our "fight, flight, or freeze" actions.

The relaxation response is characterized by:

- Lowered heart rate
- Reduced blood pressure
- Reduced breathing rate
- Lowered metabolism
- Calmer brain activity
- Increased attention and decision-making functions of the brain
- Increased inhaled nitrous oxide, which counters negative effects of the stress hormone norepinephrine (noradrenaline)
- Changes in gene activity that are the opposite of those associated with stress

In the 1960s, Benson, a cardiologist, observed his patients' blood pressures rise when they were in the doctor's office and lower when it was measured by the patient himself or herself at home or in other settings. He hypothesized that stress was a contributor to hypertension and possibly other health problems. He studied transcendental meditators, yogis, and those reciting prayers (in whatever faith or belief that was meaningful to them). He identified the common variables that one could use to alter physiological states of the mind and body. He termed this the *relaxation response* and developed a specific technique one could use to attain it. In his own words:

> My goal has always been to promote a healthy balance between self-care and more traditional approaches—medical and surgical interventions that can be magnificent and life-saving, when appropriate. However, self-care is immensely powerful in its own right. The elicitation of the relaxation response, stress management, regular exercise, good nutrition, and the power of belief all have a tremendous role to play in our healing.[1]

Based on research of long-time meditators and those able to positively alter their physiology and mental states, he created the Benson-Henry Protocol on how to induce the relaxation response and improve genetic expression to prevent and heal from disease. In my interview with him in 2013, I asked him about the receptivity of the healthcare community to embrace these approaches, and if he has seen it being taught more among healthcare professionals. Benson answered:

> The receptivity has markedly increased over the years, be-
> cause of the scientific base. And when you recognize that
> over sixty percent of visits to doctors are in the mind-body,
> stress-related realm that are poorly treated by drugs and
> surgeries, this becomes quite important. Even more import-
> ant, perhaps, from the point of view one could save money
> in healthcare, because you would be using a scientifically
> proven approach—that is the relaxation response—and
> it would decrease, we believe, office visits to physicians.
> And physicians have more and more accepted this, and
> it's now being frequently taught in medical schools.[2]

Accessing intuition often occurs in this relaxation response state, which is a meditative or peaceful state that has its own healing benefits. It may improve the immune system functioning and promote healthier gene expression so we stay well and can recover from or prevent disease. Listening to insights from your intuition may inherently put you at ease with new understandings and a sense of "this is right." You will likely experience a relief that may engage you in the relaxation response state itself. Your intuition may help you to become more confident with a stronger sense of meaning and purpose that has been correlated with positive health outcomes.[3]

Relaxing and meditative activities may help alter brainwave activity to more easily access intuition, such as in alpha and theta brain-wave states. There are five categories of brainwave states. They are expressed in cycles per second or hertz [Hz].[4]

Gamma – 25 – 100+ Hz: profound insight, peak physical experience

Beta – 12 – 25 Hz: conversation, analysis, and processing of information

Alpha – 8 – 12 Hz: relaxed, calm, and focused mind, REM sleep

Theta – 4 – 8 Hz: meditation, enhanced intuition, and creativity

Delta – 0 – 4 Hz: deep, dreamless sleep and coma

Neuroscience Research

Meditation can change structures of the brain just after eight weeks of meditating regularly. People who had never meditated before went through an eight-week mindfulness-based stress reduction program. Researchers found thickening [likely the result of the creation of new neuronal connections] in four regions:

1. the posterior cingulate, which is involved in mind wandering and self-relevance;
2. the left hippocampus, which assists in learning, cognition, memory, and emotional regulation;
3. the temporo-parietal junction, which is associated with perspective taking, empathy, and compassion; and
4. the pons, an area of the brainstem where a lot of regulatory neurotransmitters are produced.

An area that got smaller was the amygdala, the fight-or-flight part of the brain, which is important for anxiety, fear, and stress in general.

Meditation can make your brain younger. Long-term meditators have an increased amount of gray matter in the insula and sensory regions, as well as the auditory and sensory cortex. Probably because when you're mindful, you're paying attention to your breath, sounds, and the present moment. They have more gray matter in the frontal cortex, which is associated with working memory and executive decision-making. Fifty-year-old meditators had the same amount of gray matter in their prefrontal cortex as twenty-five-year-olds. The cortex shrinks with age and can cause a decrease in cognition and memory.[5]

The Power of Meditation

Meditation is one of the best ways to connect with your intuition and develop it. Have you ever tried to develop your own regular meditation practice? I have heard many people say, "I am not a good meditator" or "I tried meditation and it wasn't for me." All of the people who have told me this did not have any formal instruction or a meditation teacher or guide to help them have a more successful experience. Most of us were not taught how to feel safe with being quiet within ourselves and our consciousness.

Meditation is focused attention. In many cultures the goal of meditation is to get into a state of awareness of the realization that the personal self and the Universal Self are one.[6] There are many types of meditation. Find the style that works best for you. My intention is to support you to have a positive experience with meditation so that you find it pleasurable and look forward to your meditation time. Then, you'll be more likely to want to meditate and have a consistent practice that you will enjoy.

The more you meditate, the more easily you will likely be able to connect with your intuition. Additionally, meditation has many positive health benefits. It can regulate emotions. It can calm the mind and body, enhancing spiritual states; assist you to quiet your mental chatter, creating space between your thoughts, judgments, or worrying mind; and help return your body back toward homeostatic balance. It can lower physical and emotional pain, stress, and tension; ease depression and insomnia; create clearer awareness and insight; improve compassion, sense of well-being, and quality of life; and more.

If it could be bottled and sold, all sorts of companies would want to have the rights to meditation. But it's something you can do for yourself without a prescription, anywhere, without negative side effects.

Meditate defined:[7]

intransitive verb

1: to engage in contemplation or reflection

2: to engage in mental exercise (as concentration on one's breathing or repetition of a mantra) for the purpose of reaching a heightened level of spiritual awareness

transitive verb

1: to focus one's thoughts on: reflect on or ponder over

2: to plan or project in the mind: intend, purpose

—med·i·ta·tor noun

Modern science has caught up to what Eastern philosophies and many spiritual traditions have known and practiced for thousands of years.[8] One of the first meditation practices that made a large impact on our society was Transcendental Meditation (TM) which was brought to the United States by Maharishi Mahesh Yogi. TM is performed by repeating a mantra, a special word or phrase, for twenty minutes daily.

Today many people are partaking in the advantages of meditation. A nationwide survey found that there is widespread use of meditation and other mind-body practices. Meditation is growing in popularity and nearly 20 percent of Americans practice it—18 million adults and 927,000 children.[9]

Meditation may enhance functional abilities with Activities of Daily Living (ADL) and can be its own form of an ADL. Just like brushing our teeth or any other personal care activity, meditation can be a simple daily practice to help you connect to your intuition, thereby enhancing health, wellness, recovery, and prevention of disease. Soon you may find you're bringing the state of consciousness experienced during meditation with you throughout your daily life.

Explore the various ways to meditate to get a feel for the practices you may enjoy. Find what works best for you. You may immediately be drawn to certain styles. While there are many meditation resources and apps that can be accessed online, you may find it helpful to contact a meditation teacher or community group to help you navigate any pitfalls or answer any questions you may have. With time, you may stick with the same meditations, or you may explore other forms as you grow and change. You may want to experiment with various postures, such as sitting in a chair, on the floor, on a cushion, or you may try standing, walking, or lying down. Consider different postures if you need to mix it up or carry it into your daily life.

You may choose to develop a daily or twice-a-day meditation practice to train yourself to more easily connect with your intuition (see tips on how to begin, page 70). In my experience, meditations can fall into several categories:

- Relaxation
- Breathing—abdominal/diaphragm/belly/deep breathing
- Progressive Relaxation

- One-Pointed Meditation—focusing on a breath, word, or mantra
- Mindfulness
- Guided Meditation
- Guided Imagery/hypnosis
- Energy
- Movement—walking, dancing, yoga, qigong, t'ai chi, exercise, or through daily activities
- Prayer
- Contemplation

In addition to helping you connect to your intuition, research confirms many other health benefits of meditation. *Physically*, meditation can:

- Lower breath rate
- Lower heart rate
- Decrease brainwave activity
- Lower blood pressure
- Lower pain
- Lower metabolism
- Reduce musculoskeletal tension
- Stimulate the parasympathetic nervous system, known as rest and digest
- Elicit changes in gene activity that are the opposite of those associated with stress
- Improve the immune system
- Increase inhaled nitrous oxide, which counters the negative effects of the stress hormone norepinephrine (noradrenaline)
- Expedite healing, recovery, and prevention of illness
- Increase heart rate variability, which is correlated with positive mental states and improved health

Mentally, meditation can:

- Induce alpha, delta, and theta brainwaves
- Improve mental states to a more positive attitude and outlook on life
- Improve attention, focus, and cognitive functioning

- Decrease or slow thoughts, worry, and judgment
- Alleviate stress, anxiety, and depression
- Increase attention and decision-making
- Improve insight and judgment
- Improve planning and analyzing
- Improve creativity
- Assist personal development
- Increase detachment from thoughts and worry to become the "observer" or "witness"
- Increase attention and decision-making functions of the brain
- Improve sleep

Emotionally, it can:

- Improve mood
- Increase positive emotions
- Improve outlook on life
- Decrease emotional pain and negative emotional states
- Decrease grief, loss, or sadness
- Improve love for self and self-acceptance
- Improve relationships
- Increase love and compassion for self and others
- Increase tolerance and forgiveness
- Create a sense of calm and peace

Spiritually, it can:

- Increase connection to a greater *all* or higher power
- Improve spiritual development
- Decrease sense of isolation
- Improve intuition and inner wisdom
- Increase a sense of meaning and purpose
- Improve peace and happiness

Story

Senior year in college, I was enrolled with nineteen credits, working twenty-eight hours per week, and the stress felt like more than I could handle. To satisfy a physical education requirement, I was pleased that I could take a class on relaxation. During each relaxation class, we were guided through two, twenty-minute relaxation and meditation exercises. We listened to various recordings by Emmett Miller, MD, from his audio "Letting Go of Stress," and read selected chapters from *Comprehensive Stress Management* by Jerrold S. Greenberg, PhD.

This helped us to elicit the relaxation response. After each class, my mind was clearer, I felt more positive, and I felt lighter in my body. I walked to my next class feeling more calm and joyful with an I-can-do-this attitude. I experienced less stress and was better able to cope and concentrate on my studies.

Just a few years later, I began developing my own regular relaxation response and meditation practice, with the help of meditation teachers. By then, I had graduated with a professional degree in occupational therapy, and I was experiencing the stress of transitioning into a new career and a challenging healthcare system. As a result of my practice, my intuition and spirituality grew—and continues to grow—in ways I never could have imagined. These abilities have guided me on a more fulfilling and satisfying professional path, serving others in ways that are more aligned with my heart and soul's purpose.

Epidemic of Stress, Anxiety, and Pain

Many people find it difficult to relax and thus connect to their intuition. The stats on stress, anxiety, and physical and emotional pain, as well as substance use, have reached epidemic proportions in our society.

A 2010 Stress in America survey, conducted by the American Psychological Association (APA), found that nearly 75 percent of Americans said that their stress levels were so high that they feel unhealthy. The survey showed that Americans appear to be caught in a vicious cycle in which they manage stress in unhealthy ways, while lack of willpower and time constraints impede their ability to make lifestyle or behavioral changes. Moreover, parents underestimate both how much stress their children experience and the impact their own stress has on their children. Children as young as eight are reporting that they experience physical and emotional health consequences often associated with stress.[10]

Money and work have consistently topped the list of stressors over the past decade. In 2017, the survey revealed a new source of significant stress: the future of our nation. Symptoms of stress include anxiety, anger, and fatigue. Nearly 60 percent of adults report that current social divisiveness causes them stress. A majority of adults (59 percent) consider this the lowest point in the nation's history that they can recall. The feeling spans generations, including people who have lived through World War II, Vietnam, the Cuban missile crisis, the September 11 terrorist attacks, and high-profile mass shootings. Specific issues that cause Americans stress were:

- Healthcare (43 percent)
- The economy (35 percent)
- Trust in government (32 percent)
- Crime and hate crimes (31 percent)
- Terrorist attacks in the United States (30 percent)
- High taxes (28 percent)
- Unemployment and low wages (22 percent)
- Climate change and environmental issues (21 percent)[11]

In 2018, the survey looked at the levels of stress among members of Generation Z, those born between 1996 and 2010. Teens and young adults have become more vocal about controversies, such as gun violence, family separations, and high-profile sexual assaults that dominated the news in the previous year. Sexual harassment and gun violence were found to be significant stressors, and 75 percent of Gen Z reported mass shootings as a significant source of stress. Millennials, those born between 1981 and 1996, reported similar feelings (69 percent about mass shootings and 73 percent about school shootings or the possibility of one occurring). The youngest adults in America reported the poorest mental health of all generations. However, Gen Z is much more likely to seek professional help for mental health issues.[12]

Pain affects more Americans than diabetes, heart disease, and cancer combined. The more stress a person experiences, the more pain they may have. It is the most common reason Americans access the healthcare system; it is a leading cause of disability; and it is a major contributor to healthcare costs. Of the 9.4 million Americans who take opioids for long-term pain, 2.1 million are estimated by the National Institutes of Health to be addicted and are in danger of turning to the black market. Four out of five people with heroin-use disorder say they came to the drug from prescription painkillers.[13]

But there is hope. You can break out of the stress cycle, heal, find that peace within, and more easily connect to your intuition.

Story

Working in a hospital, I met a young man who was experiencing pain and stress from a recent surgery. He was not responding well to pain medication and was suffering terribly. His pain level was at 8/10; for stress, 6/10.

I asked him if I could guide him in a simple relaxation exercise that might help to lower his pain and stress. He said yes. I guided him in abdominal breathing, a progressive body relaxation, and a five-minute guided imagery in a special place. He imagined being in the woods near a mountain and felt more peaceful and relaxed. His pain level decreased to 4/10 and his stress level lowered to 3/10 in less than fifteen minutes.

I left him with written relaxation response instructions and guided imagery CDs. I saw him the next day, and he said he was able to manage his pain and stress and cope with his recovery by listening to the CDs and practicing the skills I had taught him. He was grateful to have learned the techniques, felt more relaxed and confident, and planned to regularly practice meditation when he left the hospital and going forward in his life.

Meditation Research

Dean Radin, PhD, the Chief Scientist at the Institute of Noetic Sciences (IONS) and Associated Distinguished Professor of Integral and Transpersonal Psychology at the California Institute of Integral Studies, has been studying the far reaches of human consciousness and psychic or "psi" phenomena for the majority of his career.[14] Intuitive experiences may also be known as psi, and he defines this as follows:

"Letter 'p' in the Greek alphabet, first letter in the word *psyche*, meaning mind or soul; refers to clairvoyance, precognition, telepathy, and psychokinesis; psi is not an acronym, it is not capitalized, and is pronounced 'sigh.'"[15]

Radin's and his colleagues' research shows that meditation can enhance psi or intuitive abilities. This mirrors others' research conducted on this topic. It seems there is more success if the meditators fully accept the experimental procedure and goals of the research. He is continuing research among those who meditate and practice yoga, with a keen interest in studying the meditation-psi-siddhi relationship as described in his book, *Supernormal: Science, Yoga, and the Evidence for Extraordinary Psychic Abilities.*

Listen to the interview: "Science, Magic, and Intuition" with Dean Radin and Emmy Vadnais: https://youtu.be/iJ4KvP9JM4o

Yoga

When you think of yoga, you may visualize the yoga poses or physical postures, also known as *asanas*. The true meaning of yoga and practice goes beyond just the physical practice, and it may help to align you with your intuition and your true self. Asanas were likely developed to help us connect to the divine within and the divine seemingly outside of ourselves. Translations of *yoga* communicate *union* or *to yoke your divine self and spiritual connection*—that is, to be connected with your inner divine self simultaneously with the greater divine and be at one. Yoga is not a religion.

> The word yoga is derived from the Sanskrit root *yuj* meaning to bind, join, attach and yoke, to direct and concentrate one's attention on, to use and apply. It also means union or communion. It is the true union of our will with the will of

God. "It thus means," says Mahadev Desai in his introduction to *The Gita according to Gandhi*, "the yoking of all the
powers of body, mind, and soul to God; it means the dis-
ciplining of the intellect, the mind, the emotions, the will,
which that yoga presupposes; it means a poise of the soul
which enables one to look at life in all its aspects evenly."

–B.K.S. IYENGAR, *LIGHT ON YOGA*[16]

There are eight limbs, or stages of yoga, that may help you with
states of consciousness, including intuition, being healthy, and living a meaningful and purposeful life. The eighth limb is a state of
absorption, known as *samadhi* (considered by many to be the goal
of yoga), where intuition may be most easily experienced. The eight
limbs of yoga are:

1. *Yama*: Universal morality
2. *Niyama*: Personal observances
3. *Asanas*: Body postures
4. *Pranayama*: Breathing exercises, and control of prana
5. *Pratyahara*: Control of the senses
6. *Dharana*: Concentration and cultivating inner perceptual
    awareness
7. *Dhyana*: Devotion, meditation on the Divine
8. *Samadhi*: Union with the Divine

The *Yoga Sutras* are a manuscript written by the Indian sage Patanjali
about two thousand years ago. (*Sutra* comes from the Sanskrit word for
thread.) The sutras are considered one of the first written documents or
threads in the fabric of an oral tradition of yoga.

The *Yoga Sutras* provide taxonomy of supernormal mental powers and means of obtaining them. Today we would
classify most of [these] *siddhis* as various forms of psychic,
or psi, phenomena. Others might be called exceptionally
precise means of controlling the mind-body relationship.

—DEAN RADIN, *SUPERNORMAL: SCIENCE, YOGA, AND THE
EVIDENCE FOR EXTRAORDINARY PSYCHIC ABILITIES*[17]

In the third book of the *Yoga Sutras* there are about twenty-five siddhis that are said to be obtained after mastering the last three steps of the eightfold path of yoga—being able to sustain concentration, meditation, and samadhi at will.

The siddhis may fall into three basic classes:

1. Exceptional mind-body control
2. Clairvoyance, the ability to gain knowledge unbound by the ordinary constraints of space or time and without the use of ordinary senses; includes precognition and telepathy
3. Psychokinesis or mind-matter interaction, the ability to directly influence matter[15]

Intuitive Development echoes yoga's teachings. If you feel drawn to begin a yoga practice, there are many studios around the world. Consider finding a teacher who teaches all eight limbs of yoga to enhance your intuition and all of the health benefits.

Meditation, through yoga, can be practiced formally in various postures. It can also be a mental exercise to enhance other daily activities and can be practiced throughout daily activities. For example, mindfulness meditation while doing any activity encourages you to be aware of what's occurring internally and externally with a nonjudging, observing awareness.

Yoga is meant to liberate oneself from destructive habits that distract the mind and create suffering, enabling one to reach a state of enlightenment. While the siddhis are important for spiritual development, Patanjali suggested that these may be natural experiences of being on the path of yoga. He advised to be careful not to get caught up in them or display them, as doing so may lead to ego, arrogance, pride, or self-aggrandizement, all of which become an impediment toward further spiritual unfoldment.[15,18] Meditation and yogic practices help transcend the ego or identification with attachments to more easily align with samadhi—that is the same as intuition.

Studies show that yoga may be able to:
- Lower stress, anxiety, pain, fatigue, depression, and insomnia
- Reduce risk for cardiovascular disease and hypertension
- Alleviate the side effects of cancer treatment
- Improve recovery from neurological conditions, such as stroke, symptoms of multiple sclerosis, and Parkinson's disease
- Prevent or lower risk of disease
- Improve a sense of overall well-being[19,20,21,22]

The asanas, meditation, or a combination of both can improve strength, flexibility, and functional mobility for a number of conditions that cause chronic pain and disability. Pain medication may be reduced or completely eliminated in certain cases. Yoga may also improve gait functioning in elders and prevent falls.[23]

Yoga and meditation practices have been shown to decrease addictive behaviors. Thoughts of self-inflicted harm and disrespect toward oneself were able to change to more loving, caring, and respectful thoughts and behaviors. Yoga has also been found helpful in recovery from eating disorders and improving poor body image.

Research shows that yoga can help reduce stress by creating the relaxation response, helping you to feel calmer, focus on the present, and decrease the stress or flight-or-fight response. It can lower blood pressure, lower cortisol levels, and increase blood flow to vital organs.[24]

Beginner's Mind

In life and when doing the suggested practices in this book, it is always helpful to have a "beginner's mind." This means to be present each time as if it were your first experience with whatever you are facing, so you're not judging it based on past experiences. Each time you practice a meditation or any activity that helps you experience the relaxation response state, you will likely have a new and unique experience. As we are all changing and evolving each moment, what may work for us now may work differently for us in the future. Ram Dass, who wrote the cult classic *Be Here Now*, said, "Be unattached to your method." Therefore, you will be open to all possibilities.

The more you stay flexibly in the present moment, the more you will be like a radio tuning in to a radio station free of static with clear reception. Then, your head and heart will be more aligned and in unison. Be receptive to what is coming and trust what you are receiving—this is your intuition in action. Play with it and perhaps journal your experience. In time, you will likely come to trust and understand how you intuit, and often draw upon this great tool that will serve you (and others) in countless ways.

Written Exercise

- When do you feel the most relaxed?
- What activities help you to feel that the "mud has settled from the water of your mind"?
- When did you have an experience where you were clear, calm, and relaxed, so that you received inspiration, creativity, or insight into a new possibility or a problem that was challenging you?

6. Develop a Meditation Practice

The quieter you become, the more you can hear.
—Ram Dass

WHEN BEGINNING A MEDITATION PRACTICE, recordings for relaxation, meditation, and guided imagery may help you get started (many are shared throughout this book). For many, having a meditation instructor teach you and be available for questions and guidance is the most helpful. You may find it beneficial to engage in some type of physical activity prior to meditation to discharge extra energy and help you connect with your body and begin to quiet your mind. Try aerobic exercise, walking, stretching, or yoga. Yoga has been traditionally practiced this way: do the postures or asanas first, then sit so you can more easily prepare for meditation. Over time, you will find the right combination of activities and a routine that will work best for you to continue with regularity. Some people find listening to sound, music, or binaural beats helpful.

How to Meditate

There are many postures to meditate in, such as sitting in a chair, on the floor, or on a cushion, standing, walking, lying down, or while going about your daily activities. Most meditations should not be practiced while driving a vehicle or engaging in any activity that requires your full attention, unless instructions specifically state it's okay to listen to or practice while driving or engaging in activities.

How to Begin

1. Select a meditation—several are given in this book:

   a. Open Heart, page 37
   b. Benson-Henry Protocol, page 72
   c. Mindfulness, page 75
   d. Lovingkindness, page 82
   e. Special Place, page 87
   f. Inner Wisdom, page 88
   g. Small Universe, page 101

2. Adjust room light and temperature, and limit noise and distractions as best you can. You may want to have a shawl or blanket in case you get cool.
3. You may play soft music to enhance the experience. Although some people find this distracting.
4. Select a posture and get into a comfortable position.
5. Begin with your breath.
6. Close your eyes or find a focus point in the room.
7. Continue with your meditation for your desired length of time.
8. Come back to the room when you're ready and open your eyes or stop focusing on a specific point.

Length of Time

When beginning your meditation practice, you may want to meditate for five to ten minutes, and then work your way up to thirty minutes. Over time you may want to meditate for up to an hour. If meditating longer than an hour, take a break each hour to stretch and move your body. However, thirty minutes to an hour is plenty of time each day. Some people find it helpful to meditate for shorter periods twice a day. Having a watch or clock nearby can help you keep track of time. Some people like having a timer. Most smartphones have this feature. If this is available, select a gentle sound to call you back to the room.

When to Meditate

Daily, find a time of day to meditate. Develop a routine of meditating the same time every day, even if you feel you only have five to ten minutes to do so. The more you meditate and experience the calm and peace within yourself, the more likely you will want to meditate longer.

Be Gentle and Patient with Yourself

Allow what will happen to happen. Do not force anything to happen or become frustrated. Let go of any preconceived ideas of what should be happening. Each meditation experience will be different. That is why it's important to have a beginner's mind (see page 67), even if you have been meditating for years.

Meditation Takes Practice, Just Like Learning Any Other Skill

If you try to make something happen (such as wanting to feel nirvana right now) or resist something that is happening (feeling tired, bored, or self-critical), you may perpetuate frustration or failure feelings; therefore accept or observe what is happening without judgment or simply allow thoughts to come and go.

When thoughts or physical or emotional feelings arise (and they will), notice and observe them without judgment. Imagine them floating away like a cloud in the sky or a leaf flowing lazily down a stream. If they return, allow them to be, and bring your focus back to your meditation. If thoughts or feelings persist, they may be trying to get your attention to tell you something. Compassionately observe what is occurring with detached and loving curiosity. These persistent thoughts or feelings may need to be processed so you can discern between your emotions and your intuition.

In the beginning, if you find it is difficult to focus for long periods of time, you may want to practice focusing on your breath to develop concentration. If you begin to feel anxious or worry, you may want to restart after ten to twenty minutes of stretching, yoga, or aerobic exercise to discharge extra energy.

Move toward acceptance, love, and compassion for yourself.

Over time, you will find a routine that will work best for you to continue with regularity. It takes practice just like learning any other skill. Be patient and gentle with yourself.

Coming back from a meditative state can be similar to waking from sleep. Journaling or drawing can be important, after-meditation practices. Repressed mental and emotional material may come to the surface while meditating.

As noted above, listen to what arises, as it may be trying to get your attention or tell you something. Doing Mindfulness Meditation (explained below on page 75) may help with your emotions, but seek professional guidance should you feel you need it.

You may have noticed that many of these approaches focus on positive feelings or stepping back from negative ones and connecting with love, joy, and peace. Play with the various approaches and meditations that can induce the relaxation response, and enjoy allowing them to help you more easily connect to your intuition.

Relaxation Response–
The Benson-Henry Protocol

The Benson-Henry Protocol, which is reprinted below, is an updated version of the original relaxation response technique, along with any additional step that teaches you how to invoke what Benson calls *remembered wellness* (often referred to as the *placebo*). This protocol is outlined in the book by Herbert Benson, MD, *Relaxation Revolution: The Science of Genetics and Mind Body Healing*. The book includes several research studies supporting how it can help heal the mind, body, and spirit, and in some cases reverse disease.

PHASE ONE: The Relaxation Response Trigger

Step 1: Pick a focus word, phrase, image, or short prayer. Or focus only on your breathing during the exercise.

Step 2: Find a quiet place and sit calmly in a comfortable position.

Step 3: Close your eyes.

Step 4: Progressively relax all your muscles.

Step 5: Breathe slowly and naturally. As you exhale, repeat or picture silently your focus word or phrase, or simply focus on your breathing rhythm.

Step 6: Assume a passive attitude. When other thoughts intrude, simply think, "Oh well," and return to your focus.

Step 7: Continue with this exercise for an average of twelve to fifteen minutes.

Step 8: Practice this technique at least once daily.

Option: Use an optional relaxation response exercise, such as repetitive aerobic exercise, yoga, meditative exercises, repetitive prayer, progressive muscle relaxation, listening to music, playing a musical instrument or singing, engaging in tasks that require "mindless" repetitive movements, such as knitting, gardening, woodworking, or being in nature, contemplating natural sights, floating on water, or taking a bath or shower.

If you take this option, incorporate three essential components:

A mental focusing device to break the pattern of everyday thoughts.

A passive, "Oh well" attitude toward distracting thoughts.

Sufficient time—an average of twelve to fifteen consecutive minutes.

Important: To ensure beneficial genetic effects, Phase One should be practiced daily for at least eight weeks. For the maximal genetic effect as established by our research, the exercise should be practiced for many years.

PHASE TWO: Visualization

Use mental imagery, such as picturing a peaceful scene in which you are free of your medical [or other challenging] condition, to engage healing expectation, belief, and memory. This second phase will usually require an average of eight to ten minutes.

Total time for Phases One and Two will be twenty to twenty-five minutes per session.[1]

Cultivating the Heart

How often do you feel compassion for yourself or others? Cultivating self-compassion, self-love, and self-acceptance can help you connect with your intuition and healing. Treat yourself with kindness, recognize your shared humanity, and be mindful when considering negative aspects of yourself.[2] This may help you find forgiveness in yourself and others.

Learning self-compassion and compassion for others can improve health and happiness. Compassion is defined as the sympathetic consciousness of others' distress, together with a desire to alleviate it.[3] This is the ability to feel what others are feeling and take action in a kind, loving way. Compassion can guide great actions and improve participation in everyday activities that you enjoy. Compassion can, in fact, be learned. Even brief training in it may strengthen brain connections for pleasure and reward, as well as lead to lasting improvements in happiness.[4]

In research, changes in brain activity were noted in people who participated in compassion training. They showed increased activity in neural networks involved in understanding the suffering of others alongside regulating emotions and positive feelings in response to a reward or goal.[5] When we are in a happier state, we are able to form more favorable perceptions, impressions, and memories of others.[6]

Many are not taught to feel compassion, and some people are so driven that they are not very kind to themselves. Five common myths of self-compassion are that it will make you complacent, and that it equates to self-pity, weakness, narcissism, and selfishness.[7] In reality, this practice can help you learn that you do not have to believe all of your thoughts and emotions. You can feel more centered by being more fully in the present moment and thus be able to better participate in activities of daily living.[2] This is what occurs in mindfulness meditation that can be carried over into everyday activities.

One way to develop compassion is to detach from everyday thoughts, emotions, and beliefs, and to connect with the part of you that can step back and observe what you are experiencing without judgment and with compassion. By stepping back and observing in a nonjudgmental and compassionate way, uncomfortable feelings, thoughts, emotions, and sensations may transform. This is known as decentering (perhaps better referred to as *recentering*). This is commonly seen in both cognitive therapy and mindfulness practices.[8] This process is deftly described in *Emotional Clearing: An East/West Guide to Releasing Negative Feelings and Awakening Unconditional Happiness* by John Ruskan.

Mindfulness Meditation

Mindfulness meditation, a term coined by John Kabat-Zinn, is being present with nonjudging awareness, allowing thoughts, feelings, and emotions to come and go without getting caught up in them. This can increase awareness, clarity, and acceptance of the present-moment reality. As mentioned earlier, mindfulness meditation has its roots in the Buddhist meditation known as *Vipassana*, which means "clear seeing" (aha, intuition!) and is similar to Christian contemplative prayer and other spiritual practices. It can create a sense of calm, peace, and acceptance.

Mindfulness can positively change how you see the world, yourself, your relationships, and other aspects of your life. Mindfulness means to be more aware of your thoughts, feelings, and experiences without having to label them as good or bad, right or wrong.

Mindfulness may be a bit of a misnomer, according to Dan Eisner, OTR/L, who practices these skills and teaches them to people at an inpatient psychiatric hospital and to clients in his private practice. He is the author of *The Clinical Success Formula,* and he says that it's about stepping back and creating space (i.e., stillness) between our thoughts. Then, we are less identified, making negative thoughts easier to manage. For example: "I am not good enough" becomes "Oh, I am having a thought about not being good enough."

Mindfulness-Based Stress Reduction (MBSR) is a popular form of meditation that is practiced in many hospitals and educational campuses. According to Bob Stahl, PhD, and Elisha Goldstein, PhD, "Mindfulness is about being fully aware of whatever is happening in the present moment, without filters or the lens of judgment."[9]

> *The highest form of intelligence is to observe*
> *yourself without judgment.*
>
> –Jiddu Krishnamurti

When you allow yourself the space and time to get quiet, your intuition or inner wisdom will speak to you more clearly. It will connect you to your true knowing that can guide you in making the best choices, improve understanding, and assist with creativity, innovation, and problem-solving in all areas of your life.

Mindfulness Benefits

Research has shown many benefits of mindfulness, including:

- It may be an effective treatment for a variety of psychological problems, and is especially effective for reducing

    a.   anxiety

    b.   depression

    c.   and stress.

- It is an effective alternative or supplement to antidepressant medication and may prevent relapses.[10,11]
- It can provide opioid-free pain relief—this is especially important for those who have a tolerance to opiate-based drugs and who are seeking other ways to reduce their pain.[12]

Mindfulness has been found useful in a broad range of chronic disorders and problems, and may enhance the ability to cope with distress and disability in everyday life. Improvements have been consistently seen across several standardized mental health measures, including psychological dimensions of quality of life scales, depression, anxiety, coping style, and other affective dimensions of disability. Improvements were also found in physical well-being, such as medical symptoms, sensory pain, physical impairment, and functional quality of life estimates.[12]

A recent study titled "Systematic Review of Mindfulness Practice for Reducing Job Burnout" found that there is strong evidence that mindfulness may reduce job burnout for healthcare practitioners and teachers. Burnout is defined as exhaustion of physical or emotional strength or motivation, usually as a result of prolonged stress or frustration.[13] Burnout may create depression; aggression; decreased commitment to patients, or clients; psychosomatic manifestations; decreased cognitive performance, motivation, and judgment; and physical and mental ailments, such as increased blood pressure, cardiovascular disease, and depression.[14]

Mindfulness meditation can be practiced for five to twenty minutes or up to an hour. Once you have practiced enough, you can bring these concepts into your activities of daily living.

1. Sit or lie down comfortably with your eyes closed.
2. Bring your awareness and your attention to your breathing.

Allow the abdomen to expand outward as you breathe in, and the abdomen to come back to your body as you breathe out.

3. Optional to practice the Progressive Relaxation (page 23).

4. Bring your focus to your heart. Allow the loving compassionate part of you to come forward; the part of you that is how you are when you're with your loved ones—loving, kind, compassionate, wise; the part of you that's nonjudging, that's unconditionally loving and unconditionally accepting.

5. When thoughts, emotions, physical feelings, body sensations, or external sounds occur, simply observe them with a non-judging, loving, kind, or compassionate attitude, accepting them, giving them the space to come and go.

6. When you notice your attention has drifted and you are becoming caught up in thoughts or feelings, simply note that the attention has drifted. Then gently bring the attention back to your breathing or what you're experiencing without judging yourself.

7. It's okay and natural for thoughts to arise and for your attention to follow them. No matter how many times this happens, just keep bringing your attention back to your breathing, or observe the thoughts, feelings, or emotions with nonjudgment, and unconditional love and acceptance . . . letting go of good or bad, right or wrong.

8. When you're ready, bring your awareness back to the room and open your eyes.

Listen to Mindfulness Meditation–Loving Yourself: https://www.youtube.com/watch?v=9osXogDGCnY

John Kabat-Zinn, PhD, developed and coined the term *mindfulness* following his experiences with *Vipassana*. Kabat-Zinn is a scientist, writer, and meditation teacher who is Professor of Medicine emeritus at the University of Massachusetts Medical School, where he founded the Mindfulness-Based Stress Reduction Clinic in 1979, and the Center for Mindfulness in Medicine, Health Care, and Society in 1995.[15]

Bob Stahl, PhD, founded and directs MBSR programs in three medical centers in the San Francisco Bay Area. He completed MBSR teacher certification at University of Massachusetts Medical Center and for more than eight years lived in a Buddhist monastery.

Elisha Goldstein, PhD, is a clinical psychologist and cofounder of the Mindfulness Center for Psychotherapy and Psychiatry. He teaches MBSR and mindfulness-based cognitive therapy (MBCT) in West Los Angeles, and is an author on the benefits of mindfulness addressing issues that include stress, anxiety, depression, addiction, adult ADHD, and success at work.[9]

> *Follow your bliss.*
> —JOSEPH CAMPBELL

Intuition can help us identify our bliss—what we love, what makes us happy—and be kind to ourselves and kind to others.

Compassion and Lovingkindness Meditations

While mindfulness meditation and MBSR have become more popular in mainstream culture and modern psychology, there are similar meditation practices known as lovingkindness meditation and compassion meditation. These meditations can increase positive affect and decrease negative affect. They involve practices of enhancing unconditional, positive emotional states of kindness and compassion.

Neuroendocrine research has found that compassion meditation may reduce stress and improve the immune response. Neuroimaging studies show that lovingkindness meditation and compassion meditation may activate areas of the brain involved in emotional processing and empathy.

Studies support the use of these strategies in clinical settings. Therefore, when combined with empirically supported treatments, such as cognitive-behavioral therapy, lovingkindness meditation, and compassion meditation, they may help target a variety of psychological challenges that are a part of interpersonal processes. These may include depression, social anxiety, marital conflict, anger, and coping with the strains of long-term caregiving.[16]

Compassion Research

David DeSteno, Professor of Psychology at Northeastern University in Boston, Massachusetts, found that people who meditate, even for brief periods of time, demonstrate more compassion in comparison to non-meditators. He notes that meditation increases responsiveness and motivation for people to relieve the suffering of others.

In DeSteno's experiment, half of the participants were taught meditation over an eight-week period that included weekly classes and home practice with guided recordings. A waiting room scene was staged by the researchers, where a visibly injured person entered, without an open seat available for them to sit in. The researchers were curious about who among the meditators and non-meditators would show compassion by giving up their seat. Actors were in the waiting room, intentionally ignoring the injured person, to create "the bystander effect," meaning that when multiple people act in a specific way, individuals typically feel pressure to do the same. In the meditation group, 50 percent of the meditators offered their chair to the injured person, in comparison to only 16 percent of the non-meditator group.

While this shows that meditation can improve compassion, and acting on it, if this experiment is representative of the greater society, we have a ways to go to be more caring toward each other. DeSteno suggests that one of the ways meditation cultivates compassion is by decreasing the "us/them" distinctions that separate people from one another.[17]

At the University of Wisconsin-Madison, researcher Richard Davidson says, "Many contemplative traditions speak of lovingkindness as the wish for happiness for others and of compassion as the wish to relieve others' suffering. Lovingkindness and compassion are central to the Dalai Lama's philosophy and mission. We wanted to see how this voluntary generation of compassion affects the brain systems involved in empathy." Davidson, who has a long-standing working relationship with the Tibetan Buddhist leader, is a neuroscientist and professor of psychiatry and psychology at UW–Madison. He is an expert on imaging the effects of meditation, and with UW–Madison associate scientist Antoine Lutz has conducted investigative research on compassion.

Davidson states that everybody—from people, including children, who may participate in bullying to people prone to recurring depression, to all of society—could benefit from such meditative practices. Through their research, Davidson and his colleagues believe that people can develop skills that promote happiness and compassion.

Sixteen monks who have cultivated compassion meditation practices participated in research along with sixteen age-matched controls with no previous training who were taught the components of compassion meditation two weeks before the brain scanning.

The participants were asked first to concentrate on loved ones, wishing them well-being and freedom from suffering. Then they were asked to generate such feelings toward all beings, without thinking about anyone in particular.

Each participant was placed in the MRI scanner at the UW–Madison Waisman Center for Brain Imaging, which Davidson directs, and asked to begin compassion meditation or refrain from it. During the procedure, they were exposed to negative and positive human vocalizations—sounds of a distressed woman, a baby laughing, and background restaurant noise—with the intention to evoke empathic responses.

The scans showed significant activity in the insula—an area of the brain correlated with bodily representations of emotion, such as heart rate and blood pressure—when the long-term meditators were generating compassion and were exposed to emotional vocalizations. The amount of insula activation was associated with the intensity of the meditation as subjectively assessed by each participant.

Another area where activity increased was in the temporal parietal juncture, particularly the right hemisphere. This area seems to be important in processing empathy, specifically when perceiving the mental and emotional state of others.

The researchers think there may be benefit to teaching compassion meditation to youngsters, especially as they approach adolescence, to help prevent bullying, aggression, and violence. It may be one of the tools to support emotional regulation for kids when they're vulnerable to going significantly off track.

Compassion meditation may promote more harmonious relationships of all kinds. "The world certainly could use a little more kindness and compassion," Davidson says.[18]

Lovingkindness Practice

Lovingkindness is a meditation practice similar to mindfulness that brings about positive attitudinal changes as it systematically develops the quality of "loving-acceptance." Both practices support you in self-healing and may act as a form of self-psychotherapy.[19]

Jack Kornfield has a PhD in clinical psychology and trained as a Buddhist monk in the monasteries of Thailand, India, and Burma. He is a renowned teacher who says that lovingkindness meditation uses words, images, and feelings to evoke lovingkindness and friendliness toward oneself and others. He has taught meditation internationally since 1974 and is one of the key teachers to introduce Buddhist mindfulness practice to the West. Kornfield cofounded the Insight Meditation Society in Barre, Massachusetts, with fellow meditation teachers Sharon Salzberg and Joseph Goldstein, and the Spirit Rock Center in Woodacre, California.

A Meditation on Lovingkindness

This meditation uses words, images, and feelings to evoke lovingkindness and friendliness toward oneself and others. With each recitation of the phrases, we are expressing intention, planting the seeds of loving wishes over and over in our heart.

With a loving heart as the background, all that we attempt, all that we encounter will open and flow more easily.

You can begin the practice of lovingkindness by meditating for fifteen or twenty minutes in a quiet place. Let yourself sit in a comfortable fashion. Let your body rest and be relaxed. Let your heart be soft. Let go of any plans and preoccupations.

Begin with yourself. Breathe gently, and recite inwardly the following traditional phrases directed to your own well-being. You begin with yourself because without loving yourself it is almost impossible to love others.

May I be filled with lovingkindness.

May I be safe from inner and outer dangers.

May I be well in body and mind.

May I be at ease and happy.

As you repeat these phrases, picture yourself as you are now, and hold that image in a heart of lovingkindness. Or perhaps you will find it easier to picture yourself as a young and beloved child. Adjust the words and images in any way you wish. Create the exact phrases that best open your heart of kindness. Repeat these phrases over and over again, letting the feelings permeate your body and mind. Practice this meditation for a number of weeks, until the sense of lovingkindness for yourself grows.

Be aware that this meditation may at times feel mechanical and awkward. It can also bring up feelings contrary to lovingkindness, feelings of irritation and anger. If this happens, it is especially important to be patient and kind toward yourself, allowing whatever arises to be received in a spirit of friendliness and kind affection.

When you feel you have established some stronger sense of lovingkindness for yourself, you can then expand your meditation to include others. After focusing on yourself for five or ten minutes, choose a benefactor, someone in your life who has loved or truly cared for you. Picture this person and carefully recite the same phrases:

May you be filled with lovingkindness.

May you be safe from inner and outer dangers.

May you be well in body and mind.

May you be at ease and happy.

Let the image and feelings you have for your benefactor support the meditation. Whether the image or feelings are clear or not does not matter. In meditation they will be subject to change. Simply continue to plant the seeds of loving wishes, repeating the phrases gently no matter what arises.

Expressing gratitude to our benefactors is a natural form of love. In fact, some people find lovingkindness for themselves so hard, they begin their practice with a benefactor. This too is fine. The rule in lovingkindness practice is to follow the way that most easily opens your heart.[20]

Excerpt from THE ART OF FORGIVENESS, LOVINGKINDNESS, AND PEACE by Jack Kornfield, copyright ©2002 by Jack Kornfield. Used by permission of Bantam Books, an imprint of Random House, a division of Penguin Random House LLC. All rights reserved.

Guided Imagery

Guided imagery is a simple way to connect to your intuition. It is a healing approach that bridges the communication between the mind, the body, and the spirit. It occurs in a relaxed, meditative state, and may also be referred to as creative visualization, mental imagery, therapeutic imagery, interactive guided imagery, guided meditation, and active imagination. It can assist in healing physical, emotional, mental, and spiritual disharmony.

A key component of guided imagery is its ability to help you connect to your inner wisdom—intuition—that can guide you in ways that are not always accessible in normal waking states. It can help get to the root of what is behind a particular challenge. This may allow for creative insights, understandings, and awareness of solutions to the most burdensome problems. It makes the subconscious more conscious. The more conscious and aware you are, the less suffering you may experience.

Often, an image can convey a meaning or symbolism far greater than we can describe in words. Before we learned verbal language we perceived the world with all of our senses and saw in images or pictures. Carl Jung created his own form of guided imagery, called active imagination. He stated in his book, *Jung on Active Imagination*, "[W]hen you concentrate on a mental picture it begins to stir, the image becomes enriched by details, it moves and develops . . . and so when we concentrate on an inner picture and when we are careful not to interrupt the natural flow of events, our unconscious will produce a series of images which make a complete story."[21]

Guided imagery is a mind-body-spirit healing approach that is expanding into mainstream healthcare as research continues to demonstrate its powerful healing effects. Research has shown that guided imagery can:

- Give a person a greater sense of control
- Increase self-confidence
- Assist with fear, panic, anxiety, helplessness, uncertainty, trauma, loss, and grief
- Increase relaxation
- Decrease depression, stress, pain, nausea, blood pressure, and respiratory difficulties
- Facilitate better preparedness before medical procedures, for better outcomes
- Decrease hospital length of stay and medication side effects
- Improve immune system
- Improve healing and recovery time
- Enhance sleep
- Strengthen connection to spirituality, meaning, and purpose in life
- Improve functional outcomes and quality of life[22]

Guided imagery encompasses all of our senses. Jeanne Achterberg, PhD, a pioneer of imagery and mind, body, spirit medicine, states that imagery is, "the thought process that invokes the senses: vision, audition, smell, taste, the sense of movement, position, and touch. It is the communication mechanism between perception, emotion, and bodily change. A major cause of both health and sickness, the image is the world's greatest healing resource. Imagery, or the stuff of the imagination, affects the body intimately on both seemingly mundane and profound levels."[23]

This is the main premise in the field of psychoneuroimmunology—how thoughts, feelings, emotions, and beliefs affect the body and the nervous and immune systems. When we experience prolonged stress or tension, we are more at risk of being unwell, as our immune systems can be compromised, and certain areas of our being may be negatively affected.

Guided imagery has its roots in shamanism, which operates much more closely to nature than mainstream healthcare. The shaman is both doctor and priest. Historically, the shaman was a bridge between the seemingly separate physical and metaphysical worlds and could help the person reconnect with their soul. Shamanism allows access to the subconscious processes underlying all of our actions, drives, dreams, and physical, mental, emotional, and spiritual limitations and freedoms. Guided imagery interacts with the interplay of the mind-body-spirit connection to create positive outcomes for health on all levels of our being.

Through guided imagery, you may discover parts of yourself you are now ready to see. This can be very enlightening, as it will give you the opportunity to connect more deeply with your true self. There may be suppressed emotions and beliefs that need to come to the surface, which may need healing or will create new insights. Your own light and love may be suppressed as well. You may find you can transform your limitations into new opportunities.

> *Throughout the history of medicine, including the shamanic*
> *healing traditions, the Greek traditions of Asclepius,*
> *Aristotle, and Hippocrates, and the folk and religious healers,*
> *the imagination has been used to diagnose disease.*
> —JEANNE ACHTERBERG, *IMAGERY IN HEALING:*
> *SHAMANISM AND MODERN MEDICINE*[23]

Guided Imagery Practice

There are many types and styles of guided imagery. Here are the first few steps that can help you more easily connect within and have a more meaningful experience, whatever your intention is. (See below.)

Listen to Special Place Guided Imagery—to clear, calm, and relax the mind and body: http://www.youtube.com/ watch?v=lgQbfEBagH8&list=UUh_kFsasrtI2F5bEhn7402A

Guided Imagery helps you to relax by visualizing and experiencing a scene with your mind's eye. It helps to slow down a whirling mind, while relaxing and revitalizing you. It is helpful to practice diaphragm breathing (page 8) and complete a progressive relaxation (page 23) prior to engaging imagery.

Allow yourself to get in a comfortable position, either sitting or lying down.

Bring your awareness to your breath and take a slow deep breath in, while expanding your abdomen, holding it for a moment, then slowly letting the air out as your abdomen comes back toward your body. Breathing in, expanding your abdomen, holding the air, then breathing out, letting your abdomen come back toward your body. Consciously relaxing your body with each breath out . . .

Now imagine being in a very special place; this can be a place you have been to before or someplace you'd like to go to. It can be a real or an imaginary place . . .

When you find yourself there, notice what you see in this place . . . Notice what part of the day it is: morning, afternoon, or evening . . . Notice what you hear . . . what you smell, what you taste, what you feel . . .

Notice how you feel being in this place . . .

Is there something you would like to do in this place? Perhaps you would like to sit or lie down to rest or just be. Or maybe you would like to walk, run, swim, or float on water . . .

Whatever you would like to do, allow yourself to enjoy doing it now . . .

You can stay in your special place as long as you like. When you are ready, begin to gently come back, bringing these calm and peaceful feelings with you, as you let the images fade, knowing you can come back to this place whenever you would like.

Listen to Inner Wisdom Imagery: http://www.youtube.com/watch ?v=3fUePTnI0Lo&list=UUh_kFsasrtI2F5bEhn7402A. You can substitute "Inner Wisdom" with Inner Healer, Inner Guide, or Spirit Guide.

Pick something in your life you would like guidance or insight about.

It is helpful to practice abdominal breathing (page 8) and complete a progressive relaxation (page 23) prior to engaging imagery.

Invite in or allow an image of an Inner Wisdom figure to come forward who is all knowing, all loving, and all wise about your situation . . . allow it to come forward in any way it would like to—it could be a wise being, an animal, an object, a flower, the wind or sun , a loving inner voice, or a current or passed loved one.

Be patient and receptive . . . if one is not coming forward, notice if one were to come forward, what would it be? Who would it be? Notice the qualities that this Inner Wisdom figure has to share with you . . . what color or shape it might be . . . what does it feel it is conveying to you . . . notice the presence or feelings it imparts to you . . . Silently within yourself, introduce yourself to the Inner Wisdom figure . . . allow it to respond . . . Ask it what it would like to be called . . . notice if it has any messages, insights, or gifts for you . . . Ask it to share information about your situation . . . allow it to respond to you in any way that is easy for you to understand . . . ask it any other question you would like . . . Take your time and allow a conversation to occur . . . receive the inner wisdom guidance or healing it has to share with you . . . communicate with your Inner Wisdom, Inner Guide, or Inner Healer for as long as you would like . . .

Thank your Inner Wisdom for coming forward and assisting you . . . bring the guidance and insights you have received back with you as you allow these images to fade . . .

Gently come back to your breath, your body . . . and come back to the room when you are ready . . .

Journal

- Journal your experiences.
- What did you notice during this experience? What information did you receive? Describe your experience.

7. Cultivate Your Energy

The day science begins to study non-physical phenomena,
it will make more progress in one decade than in
all the previous centuries of its existence.
–NIKOLA TESLA

INTUITION IS ENERGY, AND YOUR intuitive impressions may come in various forms of energy. Cultivating your energy will help you to be a clear channel to sense and receive what your intuition is telling you and discern accurate intuition from static or noise.

We are 99.9999999 percent energy. Energy consists of wave functions and invisible quantum fields. Energy vibrates. It is light and particles. As mentioned earlier in Chapter 3, quantum physics tells us that everything is made of energy, including humans. Your body, emotions, and spirit—YOU—are all energy. What you may think of as a physical feeling is the electromagnetic force of electrons pushing away their electrons.[1]

We are alive and able to move around because of the energy we have. Energy may be thought of as a blueprint of your physical, mental, emotional, and spiritual being that runs through, around, and emanates from your soul or body.

A simple way to understand energy is to think in terms of our everyday language. For example, someone might say, "the room had a lot of energy," "my energy is down," or "she seemed really up." You may notice how much energy you have by how you feel inside your body and whether you're feeling "full of energy," "spent," or just "so-so." You may notice that being in a particular environment such as nature "restores your energy reserves." Being with a particular person or group can leave you feeling "drained" or it may "lift your spirits or energy."

Take a moment and feel yourself in your physical body. Take a few breaths and notice where in your body you feel the most alive, calm, centered, or peaceful. This is where your energy is likely flowing the most. Where do you feel tight, constricted, in pain, or discomfort? This is likely where your energy is restricted.

Everything has the potential to affect your energy. Your energy can become up, down, depleted, blocked, or even excessive due to:

- Family lineage/DNA
- What you eat or drink
- Your thoughts, emotions, belief patterns
- How much or little you "do" in a day
- The activities you participate in and your activity level in relationship to your rest
- The environment (including the universe)
- Relationships to yourself/others
- Where and with whom you spend time
- Your relationship with your higher power

How you are feeling can be directly related to your emotions that, in addition to biochemistry (that is energy), carry their own form of energy. Your energy can be impacted if you're feeling sad, happy, angry, or fearful.

You can learn to cultivate, balance, heal, and increase the flow of your energy. Energy healing has been used in all cultures for many years. In some cultures, it has its root in healing temples where "laying on of hands" was practiced: a person receives divine life force channeled through the energy healer. It has likely been around as long as humans were aware of energy and how it may positively affect health and well-being. But this ancient science thrives in modern times.

Cultivating your energy and bringing it into balance so it may flow harmoniously may help you:

- Feel vital, well, and live life to the fullest
- Get to the core of who you are
- Get to the root of what may be causing symptoms, disease, or dis-harmony within and in relation to all aspects of your life
- Recover or heal from an illness
- Enhance the functioning of the physical body as the shifts in energy are the foundation for the physical body
- Prevent illness or stay well
- Enhance the mind and mental health as changes in energy may create a sense of calm, relaxation, and sense of well-being
- Improve your connection to spirituality, higher power, God, or higher self as it conjures up a connection to something that is not easily seen or understood with our rational, logical, and linear minds
- And more

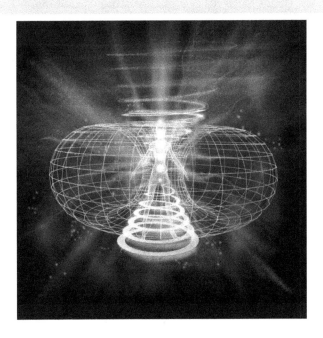

Intuition is what is primarily used when sensing your own and others' energy in order to direct healing energy. Energy healing can be easily practiced anywhere as no special tools are required—only an open, loving, and compassionate heart of the practitioner. You can receive support as a recipient of energy healing or learn how to sense, cultivate, and harmonize your own energy.

People who are attuned to energy, such as shamans, acupuncturists, and energy healers, have been able to detect an energy field that we emit, also known as an *aura*. This comprises our internal energy that we're born with—DNA—what we eat, and our level of consciousness or awareness mixed with the energy of the earth and the heavens that run through us and around us. Many energy healing practitioners work with light and are sometimes referred to as *light workers*.

Currently, energy healing is being increasingly used in hospitals, clinics, and private healthcare practices, and in certain cases it may decrease length of stay. A person still may need physical movement or exercises, or even surgery, but the energy healing may help heal what is at the core of the imbalance in the first place.

Chakra (from Sanskrit: *chakras*, meaning "Spinning Wheels of Light") seems to be a psychic energy vortex that aligns and intermingles with the spine, nervous system, and glands. As we saw earlier, the heart is one of the chakras and emanates a frequency. Chakras may have been

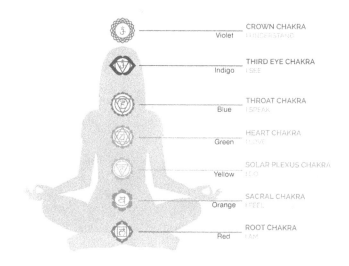

first described by the ancient Aryan culture that recorded them in India's oldest written text, the *Vedas*, 1200-200 BCE. They are considered to be the truth by the Hindus and are linked to yoga. Some traditions say there are more chakras—such as nine or twelve—than the seven traditionally addressed in Western culture. Vajrayana Buddhism proposes only five. However, since chakras are a vortex where energy can come in and out of the body, there may be no limit to how many there are. It is suggested to master your understanding of the seven-chakra system before adding more.[2,3,4] In addition to the seven chakras, healing and spiritual traditions from various cultures teach us that we have energy openings in the palms of our hands and the soles of our feet.

According to Traditional Chinese Medicine that has been practiced for more than two thousand years, there are fourteen main energy meridians that flow through your body and connect to all of your internal organ systems. These can be seen on an acupuncture chart. There are close to two thousand acupoints along these meridians. This is where an acupuncturist will insert needles or apply acupressure to help align the energy.

An energy healing practitioner can assess all of the components that make up your energy system and help it flow more properly by directing energy for healing. There may be areas where the energy is depleted or weak. It may be too strong or powerful, or there may be

Chakra	Also Known As	Color	Tone	Gland	Body Area	When Balanced
Chakra 7	Crown	Violet	B	Pineal	Top of Head, Brain	One with All
Chakra 6	Third Eye	Indigo	A	Pituitary	Head, Brain, Forehead	Intuition, Mental Process, Wisdom
Chakra 5	Throat	Blue	G	Thyroid	Throat, Neck, Base of Head	Expressing Truth to Self and Others
Chakra 4	Heart	Green	F	Thymus	Heart, Lungs, Shoulders, Arms, Diaphragm, Rib Cage/Thoracic Spine	Love, Joy, Peace, Gratitude, Bridge Between Heaven and Earth
Chakra 3	Solar Plexus	Yellow	E	Pancreas	Pancreas, Spleen, Stomach, Liver, Gallbladder, Portion of Large and Small Intestine, Thoracolumbar Spine	Will, Self Esteem Ability to Move Forward, Personal Power
Chakra 2	Sacral	Orange	D	Adrenals	Upper Pelvis, Reproductive Organs, Kidneys Portion of Large and Small Intestine, Sacrum	Creativity, DNA Sexuality, Finances
Chakra 1	Root	Red	C	Gonads	Lower Pelvis, Hips, Legs, Knees, Feet, Tail	Family, Tribe, Physical Security

blocks where the energy is not flowing well. When seeking an energy healing practitioner, check out their background or ask them where they received their training. It's best if they have received certification through a qigong, reiki, therapeutic touch, or Healing Touch program. You can also ask them about their experience working with your area of intention, problem, or concern.

Energy Healing Styles

There are many styles of energy healing. All of them may help return the energy back to balance or homeostasis. Some forms use touch and some use non-touch or a combination. Qigong, reiki, Healing Touch, and therapeutic touch use no touch or very light pressure on the body to balance the flow of energy in and around the body of the recipient. The energy healer may use their hands and intuition to assess where the energy is flowing, blocked, or stagnant. They may move their hands above and around the recipient's body to remove unwanted energy, bring in, and align the energy system.

Acupressure, craniosacral therapy, massage therapy, reflexology, and other healing approaches address the whole person's positive energy healing; they may stimulate or sedate the energy system through gentle touch and pressure. In his book, *Acupressure for Emotional Healing: A Self-Care Guide for Trauma, Stress, and Common Emotional Imbalances*, Michael Reed Gach, PhD, founder of the Acupressure Institute, states that acupressure extends far back in history to more than five thousand years ago. Chinese healers found that applying pressure with their fingers and hands to specific points on the body could relieve pain, alleviate physical symptoms, benefit the function of internal organs, and balance emotions.

T'ai chi or yoga may help open and balance the energy system through gentle stretching and elongation of soft tissue with toning and strengthening. Acupuncture uses needles to remove restrictions for health and wellness. Additional energy healing principles that can transform limiting thoughts, beliefs, feelings, and emotions, and open to positive outcomes include: guided imagery, somato-emotional release (*soma* meaning body), Emotional Freedom Technique (EFT), Hakomi, and

BodyTalk. Flower essences, essential oils (aromatherapy), and homeopathy may also support your energetic health.

If you have never experienced an energy healing session, give it a try. You might open a doorway that may truly transform areas in your life in unique and wonderful ways. Having an energy healing session can be very calming and insightful. All energy healers have a unique style. We are trained to use all of our senses to assess your energy and restore it to balance.

You can connect with your own vital life force through energy practices and meditations. You can learn daily practices that can assist you for a lifetime. Some of these approaches involve gentle movements, such as qigong, t'ai chi (a form of qigong), or yoga. Qigong and yoga share similarities in their intention to align you with yin (earth) and yang (heaven), the inner and the outer cosmos or universe, and the qualities of the feminine and the masculine.

Some of these practices are simple breathing techniques, and some of them are meditation practices using imagery to direct and guide your own energy in and around you. Learning about your energy system directly links you to your intuition, which can guide you in all aspects of your life. This knowledge can also strengthen your spirituality and connection to your God or higher power, if so desired.

When I first heard of energy healing, I thought it was not real. After studying, practicing, receiving it, and looking at research for more than twenty years, I know it's real. I often begin my sessions with an energy assessment using my intuition. This informs me where the energy is flowing or is restricted in a person's being. This gives me direction on the best tools, techniques, and guidance I can provide my client for the optimum healing results.

I was trained in medical qigong. My teacher trained with qigong masters in China and brought this knowledge to the U.S. *Qigong* means "energy movement." I learned to feel with my hands, intuition, and all my senses, detecting where the energy was flowing or constricted in and around the body and how to assist the energy to flow more easily. I learned to assess the meridians of acupuncture, the aura, and the chakras. I learned self-healing meditations that I often teach to my clients and students in classes.

I like to see and feel where the energy is flowing well and what areas need more connection. I often perceive energy in a form of white or golden light. Seeing images and hearing words or messages also gives me insight into where the energy is flowing well, where it may be lacking or too much, or where it is constricted and what areas need to be addressed. I often use a combination of on- and off-body techniques with touch—bodywork or manual therapy—along with guided meditation, guided imagery, and EFT, as energy can express itself as emotions in the body and can be held in the body. The energy is encouraged to return to a harmonious balance.

Over many years of providing energy healing in hospitals, skilled nursing facilities, private practice, and classes, I am convinced of its ability to be an effective assessment tool. It promotes understanding of the core of what is flowing and harmonious for an individual, as well as what areas need assistance, especially related to restoring health. Assessing with energy healing allows a practitioner to get to the core of what may be limiting someone that may not be so readily evident or knowable through health history, interviews, or other assessments.

Energy Healing Research

When I am helping a person to relax by guiding them to imagine they are at a special place, nine times out of ten they pick a place in nature. It makes sense that we would feel most comfortable on the earth, surrounded by flowers, plants, trees, water, mountains, forests, or rolling hills since we *are* nature. Our bodies are made of what is found in the earth, stars, and cosmos.

Connecting with nature seems good for us. *Grounding* (or *earthing*) is a term used to describe having your bare feet completely placed on the ground. Research supports that grounding the human body to the earth may be essential to health, along with sunshine, clean air and water, nutritious food, and physical activity. Earthing may be a potential treatment for a variety of chronic degenerative diseases. A study, "Earthing: Health Implications of Reconnecting the Human Body to the Earth's Surface Electrons," showed that "when the body is grounded, its electrical potential becomes equalized with the earth's electrical potential through a transfer of electrons from the earth to the body." The study confirms the "umbrella" effect of earthing the body explained by Nobel Prize winner Richard Feynman in his lectures on electromagnetism.[5] Feynman said that when the body potential is the same as the earth's electric potential (and thus grounded), it becomes an extension of the earth's gigantic electric system. Simply making contact with the earth by being either outside barefoot or connected to grounded conductive systems while indoors, may be a natural and "profoundly effective environmental strategy" against chronic stress, ANS (autonomic nervous system) dysfunction, inflammation, pain, poor sleep, disturbed HRV (heart rate variability), hyper-coagulable blood, and many common health disorders, including cardiovascular disease."[6]

Energy healing is noninvasive with little risk to people. Several well-designed studies have shown significant outcomes for wound healing and advanced AIDS, as well as positive results for pain and anxiety, among other conditions. It may have positive effects on or-thopaedic conditions, including fracture healing, arthritis, and mus-cle and connective tissue.[7]

A reiki study of 118 cancer patients, 67 women and 51 men with a mean age of 55 years old, who were receiving chemotherapy, also received one to four reiki sessions that lasted about 30 minutes each. Their pain and anxiety levels were scored on a numeric rating scale with a description of the physical feelings by the reiki practitioners. The mean anxiety score decreased from 6.77 to 2.28 ($P <.000001$) and the mean pain score from 4.4 to 2.32 ($P = .091$). The sessions were found to be helpful in improving well-being, relaxation, pain relief, sleep quality, and reducing anxiety. Reiki may help a person's physical and emotional needs.[8]

Several studies suggest that acupuncture may help reduce chronic pain, such as low-back pain, neck pain, and osteoarthritis/knee pain. It may help decrease the frequency of tension headaches and prevent migraine headaches. There are varied clinical practice guidelines and recommendations about acupuncture.[9]

The energy system may be more complex than current technological devices can detect. One way that energy is detected on a living organism is by measuring electrical conductivity of the skin. There are several commercially available instruments that do this with limited information about their "scientific" reliability. One study quantified measurement variability and assessed reliability of a device, the AcuGraph system, that is a commonly used electrodermal screening device.

The study determined that the device measures known resistors and organic matter accurately and reliably and that skin conductance at acupoints that were recorded by one operator were also reliable. The inter-rater reliability—use of different operators of the device—was less consistent and operator training and technical improvements to the device may improve consistency with operators.[10]

Some skeptics may argue there has not been a consistent way to effectively measure a person's energy with technology. Technology and science, as we commonly know it, may not be the best technique to assess human energy. More reliance on our intuition may help us to understand these areas.

Stories

I became convinced of energy healing's veracity when teachers who provided energy healing for me were able to mirror back what was happening and how I felt in my consciousness, body, emotions, and spirit, without me verbally telling them. After every session I felt more relaxed, connected, balanced, positive, and optimistic. I found I was able to do the same for others during my qigong training when people would come to our free clinic. I would assess their energy—aura and meridians—with my intuition. It was often the case that the meridians that were not flowing well were a metaphor for what was happening in a person's life or were already affecting them physically.

For example, with one man I found that the energy of his spleen and kidney meridians was weak. I was able to help it flow more by channeling energy from the universe per my training. I shared with him that it didn't mean there was anything wrong with those organs but that it may be a metaphor from Traditional Chinese Medicine. He confirmed that he was under significant stress (kidney) with a new job and upcoming move, and he was not eating and digesting well (spleen). After our session, he said he felt more hopeful and had a better mindset to cope with the changes.

The metaphors for meridians and their corresponding organ systems are more complex than allopathic medicine understands by merely viewing the body as a physical machine. Nevertheless, if there are ongoing physical, mental, or emotional signs and symptoms of concern, I refer the person back to their primary care practitioner to be evaluated and treated if needed.

While working in the hospital and in private practice I have taught caregivers of loved ones who were experiencing cancer, cardiovascular disease, paralysis, or other illnesses. These people often felt helpless about how to help their loved ones feel better, cope, and heal in the most optimal way. This helped the caregiver feel like they had tools to help their loved one, and the person receiving the care felt their love, care, and energy flow. They often reported feeling more calm and relaxed, less anxious, and less physical pain. Many of the caregivers easily sensed the energy, and the recipients reported being able to feel the energy moving in and around them with decreased symptoms.

One day, I was on the oncology unit having my third visit with a man who was in for a stem-cell transplant. On the prior visits, I had helped him lower his pain and nausea with energy healing and foot reflexology. While this had helped him, he was still somewhat uncomfortable and significantly lethargic. I taught his sister and brother-in-law how to provide him the "heaven-earth" energy healing with their hands, mind, and heart (sometimes referred to as a *chakra connection*). It was a beautiful experience to see all three of their energies connect together with universal or divine energy in a loving way, and to see the man's energy improve as well as that of his loved ones. The relatives were grateful to have a way to help their brother feel better. He described feeling more light in his body and mind, as well as full of love and gratitude for being so deeply supported. His loved ones now have a tool that can help when other healthcare professionals are unavailable. In addition, they can assist others with their energy in positive ways.

Energy Flows Where Attention Goes

You can learn to sense, direct, cleanse, balance, or harmonize your own energy. Below are three energy practices for self-healing, and I recommend you begin by sensing the energy ball. Then move to the Small Universe Meditation (explained below) to connect with the heaven and earth energies. Positively affect your chakras with the chakra meditation.

Energy Ball

1. *Sit in a comfortable position.*
2. *Face the palms of your hands toward each other, as if you're holding a ball.*
3. *Breathe in and let your arms expand out.*
4. *Breathe out and let your arms and hands come back toward each other without physically touching. Repeat steps 3 and 4 until you feel as though you're holding a balloon in your hands.*
5. *Pulse your hands back and forth until you feel a slight*

resistance, like two magnets resisting each other.

6. *Play with your energy ball, making it as large or as small as you like.*

7. *Place your hands with this energy anywhere on your body where you would like to receive some support and healing energy. Rest them there for as long as you like, absorbing this cultivated qi.*

Listen to Small Universe Meditation: http://www.youtube.com /watch?v=dAa7S2YVCc8&list=UUh_kFsasrtI2F5bEhn7402A

This qigong meditation is helpful on many levels. It cultivates your whole human energy field, or aura. It connects you to the heaven (*yang*) and earth (*yin*) energies. It strengthens the conception (*ren*) and governing (*du*) meridians or energy channels located on the front and back of your body; it corresponds with the chakras or main energy centers of the body. These channels connect with all of the other meridians of the body and organs. This is a very grounding, centering, and healing meditation.

Heaven-Earth

1. *Sit in a chair, with your hands on your lap and palms facing up, feet shoulder-width apart and flat on the floor.*

2. *Allow yourself to be comfortable. Position a pillow on your back if needed.*

3. *Rest the tip of your tongue on the roof of your mouth, just behind the front teeth (this loosens the jaw and connects energy). Imagine a string at the top of your head gently pulling you upright.*

4. *Close your eyes and become aware of your breath. Take a few slow, deep breaths in and out. Allowing your belly to expand with each breath in and return toward your body with each breath out (diaphragm breathing).*

5. *Become aware of your feet and your connection to the earth's energy, feeling it as feminine energy.*

6. *Bring the earth's energy up through the center of your feet.*

> *Visualize the energy, feel and connect with it. Feeling it as feminine energy.*

7. *Allow the earth's energy to continue to travel from your feet, through your lower legs, knees, upper legs, hips, and pelvis.*

8. *Allow the Earth's energy to come up the center of your legs, through the perineum, at the base of your spine, and up the center of your body through the abdomen, diaphragm, and chest. Let it move across your shoulders and down your upper arms, elbows, into your forearms, wrists, and out the palms of your hands.*

9. *Bring your awareness to your chest and allow the energy to move up through your throat, through the center of your head, and out the top of your head.*

10. *Let this energy shower down around the sides of you, the front and back of you, and back to the earth, underneath you, encapsulating you.*

11. *Bring your attention to the top of your head.*

12. *Become aware of heaven's energy and your connection to it, feeling it as masculine energy.*

13. *Allow heaven's energy to come into the center of your head, moving down through your head into your throat area.*

14. *Allow heaven's energy to come into the palms of your hands, moving up through your wrists, forearms, elbows, upper arms, shoulders, and connecting at the throat.*

15. *Let heaven's energy move into your chest, diaphragm, abdomen, pelvis, through your perineum, and into the earth. Allow it to move from your pelvis into the hips, down the upper legs, knees, lower legs, ankles, and feet, into the earth and back up around the sides of you and the front and back of you, over your head, encapsulating you.*

16. *All the while, heaven and earth energies are moving simultaneously.*

The Orbit

17. *Bring your awareness to the location of your* tan tien *(pronounced* dan tien*), about two and a half inches below your navel.*

18. *Bring the energy from your tan tien down to the perineum, up the back of your pelvis, through your spine to your lower back, middle back, upper back, back of neck, base of head, back of head, up to top of head, down through the forehead, center of your eyes, nose, around the mouth, to chin, throat, chest or heart area, diaphragm, and back to your abdomen at the tan tien.*

19. *Run the orbit at least two times.*

20. *Feel yourself in your energy field. Notice the areas where it is more difficult to see, feel, or connect with the energy. This is where your energy may be blocked. You may wish to focus on those areas to connect the energy.*

21. *You may begin to feel the orbit rotating smoothly as your energy moves more freely and you become more centered and connected.*

Journal your experience.

Listen to Chakra Meditation: http://www.youtube.comwatch?v =nrWzGju23H4&list=UUh_kFsasrtI2F5bEhn7402A

Begin with your breath, taking a few slow deep breaths in and out.

Bring your awareness to your **first chakra**, *located at the base of your spine or your perineum.*

When focusing on this part of you, notice what comes forward.

Using all of your five senses in this area, notice what you might see, smell, hear, taste, or feel. Notice what feelings may be coming forward; are you experiencing tension, any emotions in this area, a feeling of being closed, protective, or open?

Perhaps you're feeling joy, fear, sadness, anger, or love—just notice what's coming forward. What might this part of you be communicating to you?

There may be times when we feel nothing is coming forward. If so, just hang out with that blankness or feeling of nothingness, and observe what emotions might come forward—or perhaps it's covering something up. We don't want to push past this; bring love and compassion to this part of you, not trying to push past anything or make anything happen. Just let things unfold as they will, and come forward as they will. What does this part of you seem to be communicating to you?

Repeat this process, moving to your **second chakra**, *located just below your belly button.*

Now move to your **third chakra**, *located at the center of your abdomen, just below the sternum.*

Now proceed to your **fourth chakra**, *located in the center of your chest, in your heart area.*

Continue to your **fifth chakra**, *located at your throat area.*

Move to your **sixth chakra**, *located at the forehead, the area between your eyes.*

Finally move to your **seventh chakra**, *at the top of your head.*

When focusing on each chakra, become aware of:

- *What do you notice when focusing in this area?*
- *What do you sense with your five senses?*
- *What might you see, smell, hear, taste, or feel?*
- *What qualities does it have?*
- *What do you notice about the details: what color, shape, and texture does it have?*
- *How do you feel when focusing on this area?*
- *Do you experience joy, fear, anger, or love?*
- *What does it convey to you or what may it be communicating to you?*
- *What does this part of you need?*

Bring love, compassion, understanding, and acceptance to this part of you.

The above questions can be used when connecting with any part of your being or body.

You may find it helpful to journal, draw, or paint messages or images that have come forward, and to correlate each message, image, or feeling with the meaning of each chakra. This will help you to further understand what these parts of you want you to know and understand to assist you in all aspects of your life, and to balance and align your mind, body, and spirit.

8. The Symbolic Language of Intuition

*The unconscious can be reached and expressed
only by symbols, and for this reason the process of
individuation can never do without the symbol. The
symbol is the primitive exponent of the unconscious,
but at the same time an idea that corresponds to
the highest intuitions of the conscious mind.*
–C. G. JUNG

Symbols

Intuition may come as clear and direct guidance through our senses. However, it often comes in symbols that need to be interpreted. Symbols help us communicate with our inner and outer worlds. The meanings of symbols remain flexible, even when they have universal meaning. Most important is the symbol's interpretation in context of a particular situation.

What we think can shape and create our life. We think in symbols. Before we learned verbal language, we perceived the world with all of our senses and saw in images or pictures. We still do this, even though we may not always be aware of it. Often an image can convey a meaning far greater than we can describe in words. Understanding an image can communicate and affect change in the mind and the functioning of the body through organs, tissues, and cells.[1]

Symbols or images may come to you in your thoughts, while daydreaming, or through sleeping dreams. They can derive from images you saw throughout the day that caught your attention, or they may arise when you intentionally want to have symbols communicate with you through art that you or others have created. They can come through meditation, guided imagery, prayer, or some other divinatory technique, such as tarot. You can explore symbols and images within your mind or consciousness or by looking at an image in the physical world. Drawing, writing, and dancing can give symbolic form to an experience.[2]

Symbols can easily be seen in all of the letters of the alphabet that make up the words on this page. They are seen on a dollar bill. Colors, numbers, shapes, flowers, animals—virtually anything can be a symbol or a sign to represent something or to help convey a meaning.

Symbols may communicate effectively when we are deciphering the far reaches of our psyche or soul, because intuition may be found in and is closely related to the unconscious. This is where seemingly obscure thoughts, impressions, and images reside below the surface of awareness, lost or unknown, affecting the conscious mind. This unconscious part of us seems to be aware and present, but is often split off or separate from our conscious understanding of ourselves.[3]

The more that we can access the unconscious, intuitive, symbolic, and inner parts of ourselves, the more we can understand what drives us, what serves us, what protects us, who we are, and how to reach toward our true dreams and desires. From the unconscious we can bring forth these hidden or repressed parts of ourselves to have a more complete and fully conscious understanding of ourselves and what our intuition wants us to know. We can become more integrated with all aspects of ourselves, feeling more at peace, empowered, joyful, and as healthy as possible. This is likely what Jung, the influential Swiss psychiatrist, may have meant by his term *individuation*—a process by which a person becomes a psychologically "whole," indivisible unity.[4]

Earliest Symbols

Symbols have been with us from the beginning of humanity, estimated at 3.3 million years ago. Symbols have been dreamt up by the human psyche, as evidenced in the first tools invented by premodern humans. The zigzag pattern engraved on a seashell on the island of Java in Indonesia, probably created by our ancestors, *homo erectus*, dates between 430,000 and 540,000 years ago. The next known engravings occurred 100,000 years ago by modern humans in Africa.[5]

The earliest known cave art is from 41,000 years ago: two red dots and occasional red lines accompanying them. These images or symbols were likely created by the artist pressing paint-covered fingers on the stone of the cave. The red paint was made from ochre that came from the powder of colorful rocks containing the mineral pigment iron oxide. These early humans seemed to have had a preference for the bright red ochre over other colors, and this may indicate that the color was also used symbolically.[5] It is not clear what the images stood for or why they were made. However, one can contemplate the meaning of two dots, other cave art, or any art by focusing on the images and using the *How to Interpret Symbols* steps at the end of this chapter.

Egyptian hieroglyphics are an ancient form of script, writing, and communication, full of pictures of natural and human-made objects

that have symbolic meaning and phonetic value. Considered sacred, the script was primarily used in the context of religious and ceremonial purposes.[6] *Hieroglyph* means "holy writing"—in the Greek language; *hiero* "holy" and *glypho* "writing"—and was believed to have been given by the gods.[7]

Mythology

Throughout history, from antiquity and beyond, certain stories have recurring motifs that share common themes and symbolism that convey a meaning and may be known as a myth. They have likely survived for thousands of years because they may be considered easy to identify with, and they help tell stories that explain human experience or give meaning or understanding to life.

Here is an excerpt from a conversation between journalist Bill Moyers and Joseph Campbell, author and professor of comparative mythology and religion:

Bill Moyers: "I came to understand from reading your books—*The Masks of God* or *The Hero with a Thousand Faces*, for example—that what human beings have in common is revealed in myths. Myths are stories of our search through the ages for truth, for meaning, for significance. We all need to tell our story and to understand our story. We all need to understand death and to cope with death, and we all need help in our passages from birth to life and then to death. We need for life to signify, to touch the eternal, to understand the mysterious, to find out who we are."

Joseph Campbell: "People say that what we're all seeking is a meaning for life. I don't think that's what we're really seeking. I think that what we're seeking is an experience of being alive, so that our life experiences on the purely physical plane will have resonances with our innermost being and reality, so that we actually feel the rapture of being alive. That's what it's all finally about, and that's what these clues help us to find within ourselves."

Bill Moyers: "Myths are clues?"

Joseph Campbell: "Myths are clues to the spiritual potentialities of the human life."

Bill Moyers: "What we're capable of knowing and experiencing within?"

Joseph Campbell: "Yes."

–JOSEPH CAMPBELL WITH BILL MOYERS[8]

Many myths tell stories about gods. Campbell describes a god as "the personification of a motivating power or value system that functions in human life and in the universe—the powers of your own body and nature. The myths are metaphors of spiritual potentiality in the human being, and the same powers that animate our life animate the life of our world."[7]

According to Campbell, the hero's journey is a popular myth. The hero—and this can be any gender—makes a separation from the safety of the common-day world. He then enters into an unfamiliar world full of supernatural wonder and is initiated with new experiences and knowledge. Ultimately, he returns, bestowing great gifts and benefit to his fellow people, serving them.[9]

The popular movie *Star Wars* is a classic hero's-journey story where each character symbolizes an archetype. Luke leaves his home after his aunt and uncle die and trains with a Jedi, Obi-Wan Kenobi, who teaches him about *The Force* and says this about it: "It's an energy field created by all living things. It surrounds us and penetrates us; it binds the galaxy together."[10] Supported by Yoda, the droids R2-D2 and C-3P0, and companions, including the captain of the Millennium Falcon, Han Solo and his loyal companion Chewbacca, Luke is able to rescue Princess Leia from the cruel Darth Vader. He helps the Rebellion be victorious over the Empire, restoring freedom and justice to the galaxy.[11,12]

Filmmaker George Lucas and Joseph Campbell became good friends, and Lucas acknowledged a debt to Campbell's work. Campbell said of this modernized hero story: "It's what Goethe said in *Faust* but which Lucas has dressed in modern idiom—the message that technology is not going to save us. Our computers, our tools, our machines are not enough. We have to rely on our intuition, our true being . . . [the hero's journey] is not to deny reason. To the contrary, by overcoming the dark passions, the hero symbolizes our ability to control the irrational savage within us."[8]

Archetypes

Jung proposed that we all are connected by the collective unconscious and share similar qualities called archetypes. *Archetypes* are the contents of the collective unconscious with each one consisting of similar themes and patterns of instinctual behavior. Expression of the archetypes can be seen in mythological stories or in fairy tales. Within the psyche are all of the images that have ever given rise to myths and psychic phenomena revealing the nature of the soul.[4]

An archetype may be a role that is active or predominant for you at a certain moment or during your life. There are as many archetypes as there are common situations in life. The *mother, father, child, leader, warrior, wounded healer, shadow,* and *trickster* are all examples of archetypes. Jung described the *self* archetype as the part of us that is connected to universal consciousness as a fully actualized being. He said that understanding the *anima* (female qualities in a man) and the *animus* (male qualities in a woman) archetypes—the yin and yang—is important in our growth to our whole, fully actualized, individuated self.[4]

Divination Tools

Divination tools are rich in symbolism and provide ways for us to connect with and merge universal or collective consciousness—or the divine—with our own individual minds or consciousness. These tools can help us focus and listen to our intuition and illuminate what may be occurring at a deeper level. They can provide an immediate experience of information we need to understand or learn, and guide us forward in the best possible way. Popular tools are tarot cards, the *I Ching*, runes, astrology, and numerology. Tea leaves or virtually anything can be "read" as long as one is in a receptive, higher mind and open to intuition. Meditating before using one of these tools will help you to get more out of the experience, and using them can also be a form of meditation, helping you to more deeply connect with your intuition.

I will explain a few of the divination tools that I have found helpful. While each has its own unique origins, all of the tools follow seasons and cycles of nature: spring, summer, autumn, and winter, with their corresponding elements. And each tool offers its own lens and filter through which you can look at the same focus: your own inner and outer divinity, cosmos, creativity, or God—however you frame it.

Tarot

The tarot represents the transformative, mystical, or spiritual journey of the soul. The traditional tarot chronicles the Tree of Life, also known as the Kabbalah—meaning "to receive God." There are fifty-six minor arcana and twenty-two major arcana cards within a deck with symbols, images, and art. Each card may be considered its own archetype that, when contemplated or meditated upon, may activate your awareness and consciousness toward greater wisdom.

Questions can be asked about areas of your life. After shuffling the cards with a clear intention or question, one or more cards are selected, face down, and the images on the cards mirror back what you need to know, and therefore they illuminate your consciousness. The cards do not tell you what to do, but they can give you deeper insight, understanding, and clarity into areas of your life and help you to more easily make decisions with the best possible outcome.

The tarot may help you release or transcend conflicts, conditioned patterns, or barriers to integrate and balance your material world and inner spiritual values. It may help you discover your inner truth and strengthen your true identity, inner temple, and gifts you have to give and receive in the world.[13] There are many types of "tarot," oracle, or angel cards on the market with various themes. You can even make your own cards—described in the section "Create Your Own Intuitive Cards" (see page 121).

> *The Tarot is a visual map of consciousness and a symbolic*
> *system that offers insight into professional contribution,*
> *personal motives, and spiritual development of each*
> *individual. As a map of consciousness, the Tarot represents a*
> *facet of a total life experience incorporating the "practical-*
> *everyday-world" with the spiritual growth and evolution*
> *of each person. Basically, the Tarot reflects the opportunity*
> *that each individual has to visually see that life is a process*
> *of "walking the mystical path with practical feet."*
> ANGELES ARRIEN[14]

The earliest known decks are either Egyptian or European. There is some debate on the origins of the word *tarot*. Some historians say that it may come from the Egyptian word *Ta-rosh* that means the "royal way." Others suggest that it may be an anagram for the Latin word *rota* that means "wheel with the cards," symbolizing the circle of life from birth to death. It may mean "deck of cards" from the Hungarian gypsy word *tar*, derived from the Sanskrit word, *taru*. The word "gypsy" is an old English abbreviation of *Egyptian*.[14]

I Ching

The *I Ching*, or the *Book of Changes*, has been used by the Chinese for thousands of years to explore and understand the changing present and future moments of human affairs related to health, relationships, business, politics, travel, career, social events, and inner development.

It was likely handed down from elders of the Siberian tribes that conceived Oriental and American cultures. The original authorship was attributed to a legendary ruler of China during the third millennium BCE, Fu Hsi. He may have designed the eight trigrams that, when paired, form the sixty-four hexagrams. The trigram is a symbol composed of three parallel lines that describe the evolution of things created from the duality of the yin and yang.

The yin and yang represent the duality of the cosmos. All that has been created comes from and contains the oscillating dualism of the negative yin and positive yang. This includes the protons and electrons in atoms and the conscious and subconscious of the human psyche. The dots in each opposite force represent the seeds of change. As soon as it comes into its extreme, the opposite force begins to take rise. An easy way to understand this symbol is how day (yang) and night (yin) merge from one into the other. It can also be seen in the seasons of the year with summer representing yang energy and winter being yin.

Each hexagram consists of a combination of six lines with a solid line—representing yang, and another line with two small or open lines—representing yin. Coins are tossed six times that create the hexagrams to help the inquirer with their question.

Distinguished Chinese philosophers were influenced by and influenced the *I Ching*—for instance, Lao Tzu, Mencius, Mo Tzu, Chu His, Chuang Tzu, and Confucius. Confucius used the book for his own inner development, and his writings *Ten Wings* are an important insight and treatise on the *I Ching*.[15]

> *You are the investigator, and the experiments that you make and record in this book will eventually lead to a greater understanding of the cosmos and your Self, one and the same.*
> –R. L. WING[15]

Astrology

Astrology's history dates back to eras when humans had more time and less focus on technology, looked up more often, and found patterns and

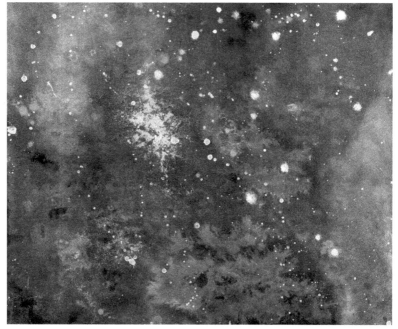

Anne Labovitz, *Under the Night Sky*, 2019,
acrylic on Tyvek®, 396" by 30"

associations with their lives in correlation to what was happening in the sky. Predating electricity, the sky and celestial bodies were a predominant wonder spectacularly lighting up the night. Astronomy and astrology were all under the same discipline. The great astronomers of the sixteenth century, including Galileo, Kepler, Copernicus, and Tycho Brahe, incorporated astrology as an important part of their discipline.

The split between astrology and astronomy occurred when it was discovered that the sun, not the earth, was at the center of the solar system, and during the Age of Enlightenment when there was doubt that human experiences were affected by planetary connections. Interest in astrology gained momentum in the 1930s and '70s with the discovery of two heavenly bodies: Pluto and Chiron, respectively. Today there is more focus on the psychological influence astrology has to offer.[16]

Astrology can be seen in your own natal or birth chart—this is a snapshot of where the planets and stars were when you were born.

Some consider it a blueprint of your soul or the potential that energies have to bring into your life. There are many symbols and mathematical relationships to understand in astrology, and it may require serious study to fully reap the benefits this system offers. Astrology is not necessarily predictive, but can show tendencies, traits, or energy that may want to be expressed at certain times over the course of a lifetime.

Most people's understanding of astrology is based on their sun sign—the constellation the sun was in when you were born. For example, you are a Taurus, a Capricorn, etc. While this is an important part of your personality, it is only a fraction of what the other planets and their signs and positions in houses have to share. The sky was divided into twelve zodiac signs with star constellations that have their own personalities. In addition, each planet carries its own qualities and actions. Where planets are placed in your chart, their mathematical relationship, and how they interact with each other paints a unique picture that may be considered to be the essence of you. Astrology highlights how the outer cosmos influences your inner cosmos (or maybe it's the other way around, or both!).

Over time, the planets keep moving and seem to continue to influence you during the course of your life. Astrology is a wonderful tool for learning more about yourself and understanding why certain interests are more or less important to you and what your soul may be trying to learn or express in this lifetime.

Intuition is a key component for a more thorough interpretation of a chart or any divination tool. Computer-generated reports may be somewhat useful, but often pale in comparison to what may be interpreted by someone trained in understanding a chart that is unique to you. Meeting with an astrologer or someone who has studied the art may be a good first step and introduction into what astrology may have to offer you.

Dreams

Dreams serve up images and feelings that may seem to be a mash-up or collage of seemingly disparate themes that, upon closer reflection, may have a congruous motif. Sometimes dreams may be crystal-clear

Nicole Hoekstra-Voves, *Unicorn*, 2018

words, images, or feelings providing specific insights or messages or precognitive content. Your dreams may share what your normal waking consciousness needs help to know.

Contemplating experiences in your dreams or keeping a dream journal may show you images or themes that are important in your life—areas in need of attention or healing. These unconscious symbols may require interpretation to gain further insight, or the overall feeling of the dream may inspire the dreamer to ponder the meaning.

There are many books and online sources to help interpret dreams. Jung, who helped people through their dreams, said that we cannot have general rules for interpreting dreams.[3] Each of us can find our own method that unlocks the door to understanding what our dreams may be trying to say to us. Or you may find it beneficial to seek support from someone who has experience working with symbols, intuition, or dreams. The following "How to Interpret Symbols" section may help you discover clues to what your dreams may be saying.

Intuition may be thought of as a daydream. It is lovely to stare out a window and just allow the mind to wander. Like a dream, this effortless stream helps you sense your intuition during the day.

Exercises that utilize dream images are provided in Chapter 9.

How to Interpret Symbols

You can explore symbols and images within your mind or consciousness, or by contemplating a visual image in the physical world. There are books and references to help you interpret meanings. However, to develop your intuition, consider spending time with the image and notice what comes to mind or what it brings up for you first. Trust your own interpretations. This is your intuition speaking to you. Use discernment and feel within. It is best to have meditated prior to following the steps below.

1. Look at a symbol, image, or picture of any kind.
2. What do you notice about the object?
3. Observe the obvious and the details: color, shape, texture, etc.
4. What qualities or characteristics does it have?
5. What does it convey to you?
6. Notice how you feel when looking at it or thinking about it; do you experience joy, fear, anger, love, etc.?
7. What do you notice with all of your senses?
8. What do you feel the image is communicating to you?
9. Sometimes it is helpful to research the meaning for a deeper understanding and awareness.
10. Discern and feel which interpretation seems right.

Writing Reflection

- *How are you "the hero" in your own story?*
- *Who has helped you along the way?*

- *Who have you helped?*
- *What are you bringing back or what have you brought back with you to help serve humanity, the planet, or its inhabitants?*
- *What symbols are meaningful to you?*

Select an image or symbol you would like to explore. Use the "How to Interpret Symbols" guide above to discover what that symbol wants to share with you. Meditate in a quiet place and let your intuition speak to you. Begin with your own interpretation before looking up information in a book, online, or other reference on symbol interpretation, which may be additionally helpful. This may help you to allow your intuition to speak to you. Use discernment and feel within. Trust your own interpretation.

Nicole Hoekstra-Voves, *Duchamp Plate*, 2018

9. Connect to Intuition with Your Own Images

To see a world in a grain of sand
And heaven in a wild flower
Hold infinity in the palm of your hand
And eternity in an hour.
—WILLIAM BLAKE

IN ADDITION TO MEDITATION, ONE of the first ways I learned how to listen to and trust my intuition was through making *intuitive cards*, also known as *symbolic cards* or *innie cards*. Intuitive cards are a tool to help you connect with your intuition so you can focus on, strengthen, and trust what *you already feel and know within yourself.* They can help you dial in to truth more quickly and cut through emotions or projections that may limit you from fully sensing your intuition. They provide visual images and words reflected back to you from your own soul that may make it easier for you to see what your intuition wants to tell you, providing insight and clarity into a variety of life situations.

I still use cards and have made new decks when it seems time for new images that want to come forward as my consciousness grows and evolves. I have had the joy of seeing many people make their own unique cards that have guided them well with developing their intuition. Of course, you can use store-bought tarot cards or other divination tools.

But to really, truly, and deeply connect with what your own psyche and soul want to tell you, I suggest beginning by making your own cards. This will help you find your own unique way that you intuit to come forward and flourish.

Making the cards requires only a little focus and attention, simple materials, and your creativity. Most people find it an enjoyable and fun process to make and play with them.

Anne Labovitz, *Pink with Turquoise*, 2019,
acrylic on canvas, 48" by 72"

Space to Connect with Intuition

Before working with your cards, meditating, or any other way of accessing your intuition, you may want to go to or create a *sacred space*. This may help you to be grounded and centered, as best you can, with your higher self in a state of neutral detachment, so you can begin to focus on and connect more easily to your intuition. Being in a meaningful place—such as somewhere in nature or a sanctuary—may help you retreat from everyday thoughts and connect more deeply to your intuition. This space could also be a special room or designated area that is clean, free of clutter and debris, where you can gather meaningful objects, art, or music. From an energetic perspective, having such a sacred space clears pathways and results in less interference in your mind, heart, and intuition.

Space clearing can also be helpful: use your intention and visualize clean, clear energy, perhaps using white or violet light, in the space you want cleared. Visualize the energy extending to the corners and permeating everywhere in the space. You may do this with meditation, prayer, or any other preparations you prefer.

Some people like to clear their space with sage or diffuse essential oils, light a candle, clap, tone with their voice, sing, or play music or an instrument. Say a prayer or blessing that is meaningful to you. If you're so inclined, invite spiritual support to assist you with clearing your space. You may wish to say:

> *I Invoke the Light of my Soul from within, I am a*
> *clear and perfect channel, the Light is my Guide.*

Or you may prefer to say:

> *Only that which is for my Highest Good and Greatest*
> *Joy, be here now. That which is not for my Highest*
> *Good and Greatest Joy, leave now. (If you are with*
> *other people, you can substitute "my" with "our.")*

Create Your Own Intuitive Cards

For this activity, blank recipe cards work great. You can begin with as few as twenty cards to get started. You'll find as you work with the cards that you will want to have more variety, and you'll likely want to make the full fifty-two cards or more.

1. In the left-hand margin of a piece of lined paper, write a list of numbers, 1 to 52.
2. Meditate or center yourself, clearing your mind.
3. Write down the first words or images that come into your mind, one word for each line.

4. On the blank cards, number each card 1–52 on the top of each card.
5. On the same side, write the corresponding word for each number on the bottom of each card.
6. Keep one side of each card blank.
7. Draw a picture or paste an image or a photograph that represents the word on each card.

The intuitive, innie, or symbolic card method is shared with permission from Betty Ann Ertwine.

Working with Intuitive Cards

The intuitive method of working with cards allows you to use your senses and intuition to interpret the cards—versus a set formula or reading an interpretation. This is an inherent method to use with your own deck that you have created. Since the images you will be working with originally came from you, there are no pre-existing guidebooks for interpretation of the images you have made.

Each card and its corresponding image will have particular meaning for you that can be accessed within you in the context of the situation

Ellen Schaefer, Intuitive Cards

you are exploring. As you work with the cards, over time, you may find they provide validation while focusing your attention on what you already know.

Maybe you want to explore a store-bought tarot or oracle deck that usually has a booklet with suggested interpretations. The core component of any modality that helps you listen within is your own intuition, and every situation is best felt and assessed with that in mind. After practice, you may find you need the cards less.

The cards are not able to predict the future or show you definite outcomes since you have free will and there are usually many factors at play as to how everything will turn out. However, they may be able to show you possible outcomes based on the current energy of the day. This may change on a given day, because of the factors mentioned above. However, they will likely show you what you may need to know or learn to be able to make the best choices in a given moment around an area of your life.

Questions

When asking your questions, be mindful to make them as clear and specific as possible. The more clear your focus, intention, or questions,

Mollie McHugh, Intuitive Cards

the better you will be able to recognize the guidance you receive. Try to reword yes-or-no questions into "open" questions, as the cards cannot make decisions for you; they can only show you tendencies, potential outcomes, and insights in a given moment.

While you are beginning to work with the cards, it is best to write your questions down so they are clear. The clearer your questions, the clearer the responses will likely be. With practice, you can formulate a question and focus on it in your mind while shuffling the deck.

Shuffling

1. Shuffle the cards.
2. Have your question, focus, or intention in mind when shuffling, simultaneously doing your best to maintain neutrality. You may want to shuffle three times to help you focus, while relaxing and maintaining neutrality. See sample questions below.
3. Spread the cards out so you can see all of them, face down.

Selecting Cards

You can pull as many or as few cards as you feel necessary. One card may give you plenty of insight. Three to five may give you a bigger picture and understanding as to what you are inquiring about.

1. Take your time when choosing a card, notice which card(s) you feel drawn to. Stay centered and relaxed.
2. Place the first card you selected on the left, working to the right. In the beginning you may wish to place them face down while maintaining neutrality as you continue selecting remaining cards.
3. You may select an additional card for clarity on one of the cards already selected.

Interpreting

1. Turn your cards over, turning them so none are upside down. Inverted cards may mean the energy is blocked somehow, but this can be distressing when you are beginning this process.

Right them for now, and in the future you can choose to pay attention to inverted cards for more subtlety to the interpretation.
2. Often it is helpful to read the cards from left to right. For example, in a three-card spread you can read left to right as past, present, future.
3. What do you notice about the image(s) on the card(s)?
4. Reference "How to Interpret Symbols" (page 117) to assist with your impressions.
5. Trust the process and what you are receiving, as doubt will confuse you.

One-card Selection

You can select one card for each question or select more than one—known as *card spreads*. Also, if you pull one card and would like to understand it more clearly, you can pull a *clarifying card* with the same intention or question in mind. One card can provide much information that you can glean about your question or focus. Give it time and really focus on the card and let it speak to you. Progress to two- and three-card spreads or more elaborate spreads with more cards, such as the chakra spread or the Celtic Cross (explained below). You may even invent your own card spreads around what you want to explore.

A simple way to begin working with the cards is to ask one of these questions:

"What is the energy around _____?" Card

"What do I need to know about _____?" Card

"What will help _____?" Card

If you find yourself wanting to ask a yes-or-no question, try rephrasing it.

Example:

"Should I take the position working at a new job?"

(This is a yes-or-no question.)

Try rephrasing it:

"What would be the likely outcome if I were to accept the new position?"

Conversely:

"What would be the likely outcome if I were to continue with my current job?"

Intuitive Card Exercise 1

1. Write the following questions—a, b, c—down in your journal, leaving three lines in between each question.
2. Ask each question and select a card.
3. Write down the card you receive for each question.
4. Take your time while interpreting the card in relation to your question.
5. Write down your interpretations.

    a. What keeps me from being me? _____ Card
    b. How can I be a better me? _____ Card
    c. How I can release old patterns or beliefs so I can be the best me? _____ Card

Intuitive Card Exercise 2

1. Identify an area in your life that may be a problem or current struggle about which you would like more clarity and understanding.

Emmy Vadnais, Intuitive Cards

2. Write down the following statement or question—a, b, c—in your journal, filling in the blanks about your situation, and leaving three lines in between each.

3. Select one card for each statement or question about your situation, filling in the blanks. Write down the card and also your interpretations.

    a.   Please give me insight into _____. Card

    b.   What do I need to know about _____? Card

    c.   How might I improve _____? Card

Two-card Spreads

Two-card spreads can help you understand two aspects to a situation. You can pull two cards for topics that seem to have two options or a duality component, and frame the duality using the suggestions below. It may be nice to then pull a third card to see how these two aspects may be able to come together or work in balance and harmony, or learn what you can do to help the situation. Duality framed as:

Choice A	Choice B
Head	Heart
Yin	Yang
Unconscious	Conscious
Challenge	Outcome

Three-card Spreads

You can really have any focus for your three cards. These below are just examples. Pull one card for each word on a row. Remember, the cards cannot make decisions for you, but can show you the energy around

Issue	Action	Outcome
Past	Present	Future
Nature of Problem	Cause	Solution
What you aspire to	What is the obstacle?	How can you overcome this?
What worked well?	What didn't work well?	Key learnings

the topic *in this moment*, and what you might need to know now. If you pull cards on another day or time, you may receive a different response, as everything is always changing.

Chakra Spread

Each chakra is a level of our being, awareness, or consciousness. Explore what is happening in each chakra—in general, about a specific topic, or to learn what may help to balance or heal one or all of your chakras. Refer to the energy healing section (page 93) for more information about the meanings of each chakra and where they are located. Pull one card for each chakra.

> 7th chakra
> 6th chakra
> 5th chakra
> 4th chakra
> 3rd chakra
> 2nd chakra
> 1st chakra

Celtic Cross[1]

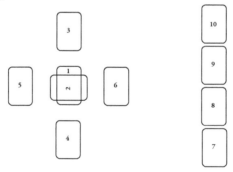

Card 1. Significator or major issue at hand
Card 2. Blocking or crossing influence
Card 3. Surface Reality
Card 4. Deep Reality
Card 5. Immediate Past
Card 6. Immediate Future
Card 7. Psychological State

Card 8. Environmental or Social State
Card 9. Hopes and Fears
Card 10. Outcome/Resolution

From the TAROT OF THE SPIRIT, Pamela Eakins, pg. 24

Scribble Drawing

If you don't have the time or desire to create intuitive cards or obtain a store-bought deck, you can create one image—by scribbling! A scribble drawing can be made in minutes and is a quick way for an image to speak to you. We began making marks as children with scribbles. They're easy and fun to make! You can focus on a question or topic, scribble, and let your unconscious create spontaneous images. This can be done with your eyes open or closed.

All you need is a blank piece of paper; the size that is generally recommended is 18 x 24 inches, although I have found 8.5 x 11 inches works as well. You can use crayons, chalk, pastels, ink paint, ink pen, or make lines with string that has been dipped in ink or paint.

1. Come up with a question, focus, or set an intention around a topic in your life.
2. Scribble for a minute or as long as you would like, with your eyes open or closed.
3. Look at your scribble art, turning it sideways and upside down until you see images, shapes, or forms that catch your eye.

Emmy Vadnais, *Love*, Scribble Drawing

4. You can make these images stronger by outlining certain lines or emphasizing them with other paints or colors.
5. You may find it helpful to describe or title your work in a way that reflects your original question or focus.
6. Let the image share with you how it answers or correlates to your question, focus, or intention by referencing "How to Interpret Symbols" on page 117.

You can also create an image, sculpture, movement, dance, or any other art form around a particular topic or intention and let it speak to you.

Dream Interpretation

Dreams are rich with images, symbols, and feelings that can be deeply reflective of what the unconscious wants us to know. However, often the information is unclear. Dreams can leave us wondering, "What

Nicole Hoekstra-Voves, *Waterfalls*, 2018

does it mean?" While there are dream symbolism books and online references that have quick interpretations, your inner self likely knows the answers, if you take some time to examine them.

Carl Jung shared that keeping a dream journal over time and looking at themes was the best way to understand what dreams may be telling you.[3] While you may want to have a bedside journal to record this rich, other world, there are a couple of simple ways to help you get further insight into what a dream may be telling you.

Dream Interpretation 1

This method uses an image and a written story of your dream that you create, where the words of the story are reshaped to a new version that gives you a fresh interpretation.

1. Draw a picture or image that represents your dream.
2. Write a summary story that describes your dream and what happened in it.
3. On another sheet of paper or document, copy your story, omitting articles, such as "a," "the," and "an." Write one word of the story on each line vertically on the left side of the page.
4. On the right side of the page, write a word that represents or describes the word already written on that line. For example, if you wrote car, write down what a car might represent to you, such as transportation, traveling, freedom, or maybe gas guzzler or polluter.
5. Rewrite your story in paragraph style, now using the words on the right side of the page.
6. Read the story with the new words while contemplating your image of your dream.
7. What does it share with you? What do you now understand that you didn't before?

Dream Interpretation 2

This method has you tap into the feeling, emotion, or interoception (felt sense) of the dream to help you gain insight and move through what the dream left you feeling. Doing so will help you realize a new, deeper and higher insight into what the dream was communicating.

This is a great technique if your dream leaves you with lingering feelings.

1. Write down in words or create an image of the feeling, emotion, or interoception that the dream made you feel.
2. Use the mindfulness meditation (p. 75) to explore and process feelings of the dream.
3. Observe the feelings from your nonjudging, witness self and notice what comes forth.
4. Keep observing any pleasant or unpleasant feelings or images that may be present until you feel you have new insight, the feelings have lessened, and you've become more peaceful.
5. If the feelings remain strong, you may need to practice mindfulness around the same feeling or themes more than one time, or use one of the above techniques.

Guided Imagery

If you prefer to work with an image within your mind instead of making a physical piece of art or representation of it, you can use the "Working with an Image" (below) guided imagery technique. This is the most fundamental and powerful aspect of guided imagery.

In a relaxed state, you will invite an image to form in your mind—it can be based on something visual or on a feeling in your body. These images or felt sensations represent your focus, intention, or inquiry. An image can help you gain insight into or represent the problem, the solution, illness or disease, symptom, relationship, emotion, feeling, physical sensation, pain, or any focus you have. Using all five senses, you can interact with the image. This can give you another perspective or deeper understanding of what the image represents. This can bring forth meaningful insight, guidance, direction, transformation, and healing.

Listen to Working with an Image—Guided Imagery: https://youtu.be/3ECTX18pBDM

Allow yourself to get in a comfortable position, sitting or lying down.

Bring your awareness to your breath and take a slow, deep breath in, while expanding your abdomen, holding it for a moment, then slowly letting the air out as your abdomen comes back toward your body. Take a few more slow, deep breaths in and out, consciously relaxing your body with each breath out.

Allow an image to form, or invite an image to come forward that represents the solution, problem, relationship, emotion or physical feeling you would like to explore. What do you notice about the image?

What qualities—size, shape, color, or feeling—does it convey?

What is the distance between you and the image?

How close or far is it from you?

Go ahead and have a conversation with the image, quietly within yourself. Say hello to the image and allow it to respond.

Ask it what it likes to be called.

This is your imagination and you can communicate with the image in any way that is easy for you to understand, through: words, feelings, telepathy, gestures, or the image giving something to you or allowing it to show you something.

How do you feel about what the image said?

Notice if the image has anything it would like to share with you.

Is there anything else you would like to ask the image or that the image has to share with you?

Begin winding down when you are ready. You can connect with this image any time by relaxing and going within or with an anchor (a hand position or physical object that may represent the image).

Thank the image for coming and allow it to fade into the background. Come back to your body, your breath, and to the room. Open your eyes (if they were closed) when you're ready.

Journal your experiences.

Automatic Writing

Automatic writing can strengthen your inner listening to your intuition, soul, higher self, or higher power.

1. Quiet yourself with a meditation, imagery, prayer, or a relaxing and calming activity.
2. Have a piece of paper and pen handy.
3. Write down a question about something you would like more insight into or understanding about.
4. Close your eyes.
5. Focus on your heart.
6. Listen.
7. Use all of your senses to notice what is coming forward.
8. Write down everything you're hearing, seeing, and feeling.
9. Keep writing until you feel you have your question answered.

In time, you will discover how you best intuit. With practice, you may find that your intuition is always accessible to you without any tools or techniques.

10. Intention and Manifestation

Whatever the mind can conceive, and
believe, the mind can achieve.
—NAPOLEON HILL

ONCE YOU HAVE GATHERED ENOUGH intuitive information, you will have a clear vision of what you want to create in your life, and you can intend to manifest it. Your intuition has likely shown you new ways to look at problems with the right solutions. You see a clear path on how to execute your goals. With this new awareness and understanding, what you want may fall into place, as if by magic.

There may be other times when you have received fresh intuitive insight, but hard-wired beliefs and subconscious patterns make it difficult to manifest it in reality. Your beliefs about your ability to achieve what it is you desire will likely need to be transformed for a positive outcome. To make it happen, you may need to create a focused action plan and follow it.

What You Think, You Become

How you spend most of your time thinking, believing, and feeling can have a direct relationship with what manifests. If you take a moment and look around at your inner and outer experiences in your life, now and in the past, you will probably see that this is true. What do you spend the most time thinking about? How do you feel most of the time?

If you recall how you accomplished previous goals and intentions, it may help you manifest what you want as you go forward. What was a goal that you achieved in your life that you are most proud of accomplishing? How did you achieve that goal? Chances are you spent a lot of time thinking about the goal, imagining what it would be like to achieve it, and took action steps to make it happen.

The *law of correspondences* is a principle that suggests that what is happening in your mind is a direct reflection of what is happening in your outer experiences in the world. Your mind and matter intermingle and interact in an interconnected reality.[1] The *law of attraction* is based on this principle.

Law of Attraction

The law of attraction states that you can create the life that you want. To get clear on what you *do* want, you need only focus on what you *don't* want. Then, feel what it would be like to have what you want, and intend or allow it to happen.

Does this sound easy? Give it a try. What is it you desire? These four steps may help you achieve it:

Four Steps to Deliberate Creation[2]

1. Discover what you don't want.
2. From that, identify what you do want.
3. Get into the *feeling* place of your want.
4. Intend—and allow—it to happen.

Positive thinking and feeling may help manifest what you want. It may or may not always be an easy task to get clear on what it is you want and maintain the positive-feeling state, especially if you have self-limiting thoughts or beliefs. A new belief and behavior may need to be created and practiced.

Can you see how you may have automatically practiced positivity in areas of your life where you have already manifested your goals? Can you see where you may be unconsciously practicing self-limiting thoughts with a negative result in areas you want to improve? Rather than focusing on your goal, you may have been dwelling on worry, negative thoughts, feelings, and beliefs—making the goal more difficult to achieve. The steps for deliberate creation are an example of how you can manifest an underlying theme of what you desire. In fact, a strong desire seems necessary for you to manifest what you want in your life.[3]

Magic

If this seems like magic, it may be. According to Dean Radin, PhD, there is scientific evidence that magic can work at times, and it has measurable results in his research. Radin looked at the history of magic and psi phenomena from a Western or European perspective in his book, *Real Magic*, and an Eastern perspective in his book, *Supernormal*.

Radin says that these abilities can be developed by entering into the state of gnosis—deep intuition—and says the best way to do this is meditation. He looked at the common features of what he refers to as magic and found that magic boils down to two basic mental skills—attention and intention—and that there are three categories of magic:[1]

1. Force of will—mental influence upon the physical world, such as prayer or affirmations
2. Divination—perception of events distant in space or time, such as accessing your intuition through meditation, intuitive cards, *I Ching*, or runes
3. Theurgy—interactions with nonphysical entities, communication with God, angels, spirits, or passed loved ones

The strength of the outcome is modulated by four factors:

1. Belief
2. Imagination
3. Emotion
4. Clarity

Clarity and Intention

You need to have a clear vision. Are you clear about what it is you want? Is it in alignment with your intuition? If not, it's necessary to really think about what you want to manifest or create in your life. If you're not clear on what you want, how can the universe deliver it to you? You may need to spend some time pondering what you want by listening to your intuition.

You need to have clear intention. As stated by the law of attraction, it can be helpful to think about what you don't want first to get clear on what you do want. What do you intend to make happen? Give yourself time to answer that question clearly.

Sometimes you may not know exactly where you are going or what your end goal is. That is when listening to your intuition can guide you one step at a time and lead you to the most amazing place—maybe a place you never dreamed was possible.

Goal Setting

You may have a clear goal and know exactly what steps you need to take to achieve it. Or there may be areas of your life that feel elusive or difficult to improve, areas that you have attempted to reach with little success. The more that your intuition and your intention are in alignment, the more likely you are to manifest it.

If you look back on your life when there was something you really wanted and it didn't happen, it's possible it was because it was not in alignment with your highest good and greatest joy, yet something better occurred. What you thought you wanted actually needed more time to develop, or there were limiting beliefs that were getting in your way, or more learning was needed to manifest it in the best way possible for you.

When I was in my occupational therapy college program, I learned how to set goals to help people with the rehabilitation and recovery process for all areas of their lives. This is a critical part of success with therapy or rehabilitation. We learned how to make clear goals using a guideline with a fun acronym: "R-U-M-B-A."

I was taught that goals must be:

Realistic—Is this something that is realistic for your life? It's good to dream big and also be realistic.

Understandable—Is your goal or intention clear?

Measurable—Is this something you can measure; meaning, how will you know you have achieved it and by when?

Believable—Is this something you believe can happen? If not, see the section on beliefs, page 152.

Achievable—Is this goal or intention something you can make happen?

Once you have set your intentions and goals, you can practice the various activities in this chapter to manifest them, while simultaneously detaching from the outcome. This does not mean not caring about the outcome. It means allowing yourself to be set free from what may be the best possible outcome given the situation. This is the same process as mindfulness.

Through the goals you work toward, you will either achieve what you set out to achieve or learn more about your intentions. You may discover more clarity about what would help you reach a goal. Usually, if a door closes, a better door will open that is more aligned with your intuition than you may have initially understood.

Over time, you can revisit your intentions to re-evaluate them and see if they are still relevant for what you want in your life. Adjust them as needed or create new intentions and goals that are more in alignment with where your life is at the moment and where you want it to go.

There may be times that your intuition points you in a direction, but you don't have a clear enough sense of what will happen at the end of the path for you to fully visualize it. You just know you need to go on that path. You know it's the right direction to take. Your intuition may not show you exactly all that you would like to know or what will be achieved at the end. Possibly you're not meant to know, because if you did, it may cause you to make other, less beneficial decisions or try to take shortcuts when the full path needs to be taken.

Focus and Attention

Where you place your attention can greatly impact your life. Focusing on your intention frequently with positive feelings and expectation may help you to manifest it more quickly. Focusing on what you want or how you would like to feel may give you pleasurable feelings and positive emotions that can further assist you in the process toward your dream and goals.

How often do you spend time, energy, and your imagination thinking and worrying about possible negative outcomes? What if you turned that negative worry toward harnessing your imagination for positive expectation? Chances are, you will likely create your desired outcome more readily.

In the suggestions below, there are many ways to give your intention positive attention. There may be certain activities that you enjoy more or that work better for you. Try them and see what works. It may be that any activity that helps you to pay attention to and focus on what you want helps its manifestation. Just like physical exercise, the best one is the one you'll actually do with regularity.

Activities to Manifest Your Intentions

Throughout this chapter there are many suggested activities that may help you transform your beliefs to positive expectations to help manifest your intention. These steps may support you toward your goal, maybe even surpassing it. I don't purport to have all of the answers, but based on research, reports from many people, and clinical experience, some of these exercises may help you. Find the ones you enjoy participating in and determine what works well for you.

Write It Down

Writing down your intention can help you get clear on what you want, and reading it frequently may help you attract what you want. Write with as much detail as you can, with the date you plan to achieve it. Read it often—once in the morning and once at night may help you draw the energy of what you want toward your intention.[4]

Take Action

How are you going to achieve your goal? Focusing on your goal and doing the above steps may manifest it. Or you may need to make a plan with action steps that you take, or perhaps there may be times you get better results if you do both.

I Sent You a Rowboat

A very religious man was once caught in rising floodwaters. He climbed onto the roof of his house and trusted God to rescue him. A neighbor came by in a canoe and said, "The waters will soon be above your house. Hop in and we'll paddle to safety."

"No thanks," replied the religious man. "I've prayed to God and I'm sure he will save me."

A short time later the police came by in a boat. "The waters will soon be above your house. Hop in and we'll take you to safety."

"No thanks," replied the religious man. "I've prayed to God and I'm sure he will save me."

A little time later a rescue services helicopter hovered overhead, let down a rope ladder, and said, "The waters will soon be above your house. Climb the ladder and we'll fly you to safety."

"No thanks," replied the religious man. "I've prayed to God and I'm sure he will save me."

All this time the floodwaters continued to rise, until soon they reached above the roof and the religious man drowned. When he arrived in heaven he demanded an audience with God. Ushered into God's throne room he said, "Lord, why am I here in heaven? I prayed for you to save me, I trusted you to save me from that flood."

"Yes, you did my child," replied the Lord. "And I sent you a canoe, a boat, and a helicopter, but you never got in."

Source: unknown.[5]

Self-Talk and Affirmations

What you say to yourself and repeat in your mind is likely what you believe. If you change what you say in your mind, you will likely come to believe the new script—that it is true, you can have it, and that it is attainable. This is known as an *autosuggestion*. *Auto*—it comes from you or is self-generated; *suggestion*—a thought or idea. As you repeat this more frequently, it is more likely that you will believe it to be true.

Affirmations are phrases you can repeat to yourself with your new thought or new belief. In order for them to work, you must believe them on some level. By repeating the words over and over, you will notice how much of you believes what you're saying. With repetition, your belief that the phrase is true will likely increase. If there are still significant parts of you that doubt your ability to achieve your intention or that your affirmation is or can be true, you may have some healing work to do to transform your belief. You can even record your intention or affirmation and listen to it daily.

Examples of positive affirmations:

"I am healthy and strong."
"I am well."
"I will stay well."
"I will always be healthy and strong."
"I can resist disease."
"I will have enough of what I need in life."
"I am enough."
"I will be taken care of."
"I will have good relationships in my life."
"I will accomplish my task of . . ."
"My life is getting better and better every day in every way."
"I give and receive love beautifully and effortlessly."
"Love will find a way."
"It will all turn out well."
"I will enjoy every moment of my life."
"I am successful."
"I will die peacefully, pain-free, and easily."
"I am grateful."
"I am love."
"I am joyful."

"I am peaceful."

Make your own. You can phrase your affirmations with, *I am—*, *I have—*, *I will—*, or any phrase that is powerful to you.

Meditation and Hypnosis

Focusing on your intention or affirmation during meditation or in the relaxation response may yield the best results. You can withdraw from distracting thoughts and emotions and are able to let your focus and intention go deeply into your subconscious. In a relaxation response or meditative state, you can use all of your senses to imagine you have achieved your goal or the experience of what you want as though it is happening now. (See Chapter 6 for detailed instructions on how to meditate and relax.)

Meditating or practicing some relaxation techniques may help your intention go more deeply into your subconscious. This may be considered self-hypnosis. Meditation and relaxation are often used in *hypnosis*. Hypnosis is getting into a light or deeply altered state of consciousness that may be synonymous with the relaxation response. This can naturally happen when you are daydreaming, looking out a window, or when you are driving yourself home; you go on autopilot, and you may not recall the last few blocks, but you make it home safely. Hypnotherapy is using hypnosis to heal or treat a condition with or without the help of a trained hypnotherapist.

See it. Believe it. Achieve it.
−Apocryphal

The only limits are, as always, those of vision.
−James Broughton

Imagery

Guided imagery, explained earlier in Chapter 6, can assist you with manifesting what you would like to achieve. It not only can help you access your intuition, it can help you use your imagination in a relaxed state to visualize and feel what it would be like to achieve your goal. This is also known as *end-result imagery* or *mental practice*.

Professional athletes use this in sports all the time to imagine getting the ball in the hoop, hole, or down the line. Research shows that imagined practice can yield better results than just physical practice alone.[6] This can also be practiced in the Benson-Henry Protocol as seen in Phase Two on page 74 that, in addition to helping you reach your goal, has many researched health-promoting benefits.[7]

Most people spend a majority of their time worrying and rehearsing negative "what-ifs." Instead, what if you turned some or all of that time into thinking about positive outcomes and manifesting them into reality? Go ahead and imagine your new thoughts and feelings. You'll find that you feel better and have a much better chance of reaching your goals.

Pray

If it is meaningful for you, you may find that prayer helps you connect to something greater, and you may use it as a time to ask for what you want in life for yourself or others, or to give thanks. How you pray, and to whom or what, are personal to you.

It's possible that prayer and a connection to a God or a higher power may be a form of its own *meaning, purpose, belief, and expectation response* (commonly referred to as the *placebo response*). Research has shown that stronger trust-based, prayer beliefs are associated with more life satisfaction over time.[8] Spiritual or religious practices, such as prayer or meditation, may lead to better health outcomes, including increased energy, longer lifespan, better coping skills, and overall quality of life during an illness.[9]

Perhaps having faith and trusting that what is unfolding is for your highest good and greatest joy will manifest exactly that in your life. Some people believe that their God or higher power knows what is best and will deliver what is best for them at the right time.

Energy healing, such as qigong, reiki, or laying on of hands may be considered a form of prayer, mental intention, or psychokinesis—a mental ability that affects physical reality. As stated earlier, energy healing has been shown in research studies to decrease stress, anxiety, pain, depression, and insomnia.

Use Symbols

Focusing on symbols that represent your intention may help you achieve it. As explained earlier (see page 46 and Chapter 8), a symbol represents something. Selecting a mental or physical representation of what you want can help you attain what you want. For example, if your intention is to have more love in your life, be more loving, or have improved relationships or intimacy, you may choose to place an object in a room or space you frequent—or wear a piece of jewelry or carry an object with you—that represents love or how you would feel if your relationship was better. A heart-shaped piece of jewelry or rose quartz are examples, since a heart shape is equated with love and rose quartz is thought to help open heart energy and increase love.

Symbolic, meaningful activities or rituals that may help you connect with your intention may involve one or more of your senses:

- Select meaningful or symbolic objects, images, or pictures and place them in a special place or a special way, such as your own altar or table in your home.
- Write or read meaningful messages, passages, or poems.
- Listen to music that makes you think of your intention or the feelings of how you will feel once it is achieved.
- Wear perfume, cologne, or essential oils that make you think of your desired goals.
- Declutter by removing objects, images, pictures, or clothing that doesn't feel useful or bring you joy, thereby making room for new energy to come in your life related to your goals.
- Review the activities in Chapter 8. What other personally meaningful activities can you think of to help manifest your goal?

Create a Vision Board

A vision board or dream board can be made with poster board and any images, words, or objects that represent what it is you want in your life. Here is how to create your vision board.

Supplies needed:

- Poster board, 11 x 14 inches or any other size and paper of your personal preference

- Scissors
- Glue stick
- Colored pens, markers, or pencils
- Photos, images, or small objects representing what you want in your life (old magazines can also be cut up)

Method:
- Find images or objects that represent what you would like to have or experience in your life.
- Glue items wherever you would like on the board, perhaps even creating a collage.
- Post words that represent your desire and intention. You can clip them from a magazine or write them with pen, pencil, or marker.
- Let the board dry.
- Place your board where you will see it often or every day.
- Experience the feelings the images give you.
- Imagine how good it would feel to achieve your goal.
- Notice how what you have placed on your board begins to manifest in your life in ways that support your goal or intentions.

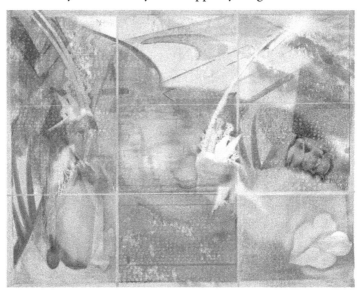

Nicole Hoekstra-Voves, *Horses Collage*, 2016

Emotion

Getting into a feeling state with positive emotions of how wonderful it would be to have achieved your intention may help it manifest more easily. Perhaps getting into a feeling state that matches the energy of what you want helps draw like energy to you. Go ahead and let yourself dream about what you want, feel the deep desire, and think about it and feel how fantastic it would be to have.

The intensity of your desire may help invite what you want. Intuition may burn so fervidly that you feel anxious or stressed if you don't follow it. You just know that its direction is right for you, and no other path will do. Therefore, it may feel like it is bound to happen!

On the flip side, you may experience some doubt, fear, unworthiness, or another negative emotion, thought, or belief when focusing on your intention or ideal outcome. Some of that may be minimal and can change as you focus more on what you want, drawing it toward you. However, if you experience so much negative expectation that it keeps you from getting into a positive feeling state about your ability to attain your intention, you may have some beliefs that need to be transformed. Your emotions may dictate your beliefs. These limiting beliefs may need attention and healing. Healing emotions can help heal thoughts and form new positive expectations and beliefs for you to reach your goals.

Experiencing gratitude for what you have already manifested or what you would like to manifest may help you achieve a positive state to help you achieve your goals; in addition, gratitude has many previously mentioned health benefits. It is natural to want to improve your life and make things better. Notice how what you want may enhance your life while noticing the good that is presently happening in your life.

At any given moment, there is likely much that you can be grateful for: your ability to see beauty in nature or someone's eyes, hear transcendent music, or taste delicious food. Maybe you recently had a good laugh with a friend or gave or received a smile from someone passing you on the street. Perhaps you have a few moments to look up in the sky and be grateful for the wonder of the universe. You may even relish the experience of just being alive.

Steps that may increase a sense of gratitude and well-being:[10]

- Journal about things for which to be grateful.
- Think about someone for whom you are grateful.
- Write and send a letter to someone for whom you are grateful.
- Meditate on gratitude (this may connect you to present-moment awareness).
- Undertake the "Count Your Blessings" exercise (at the end of the week, write down three things for which you were grateful).
- Practice saying "thank you" in a sincere and meaningful way.
- Write thank you notes.
- If spiritual or religious, pray about your gratitude.

> *What you appreciate, appreciates.*
> –Lynne Twist

Believe

It's important that you believe your goal or intention is possible. If you don't, it's less likely to happen. Your thoughts and beliefs may be impacting your ability to reach your goals. Sometimes the very fact you believe you cannot do something or have something may preclude you from being able to do or have it.

To trust your intuition in the first place, you must believe you *can* trust it. It's necessary to believe that new thoughts from your intuition are true and any related goals you have are achievable. You need to believe this on all levels within yourself and trust that it will occur. If there is any doubt, you may want to revisit your intuition and spend more time really listening to it. If it keeps giving you the same guidance, and it's hard to believe you can achieve this, then you may have limiting beliefs that need to be transformed. Listening to your intuition and changing your mind may help you open to what you want. This may help you transform a belief about your ability to have what you want. The very act of connecting with your intuition and engaging in new positive emotions, thoughts, and behaviors may naturally transform some of your limiting beliefs. This connection will help you with manifestation.

However, if your limiting beliefs are strong, you may need additional ways to help new positive beliefs form to replace the negative beliefs.

Belief often exists in the subconscious or unconscious mind, below your surface of awareness and everyday thoughts. What you believe can be brought to the conscious mind to work in your favor. Your conscious and subconscious both need to be aligned for something to manifest.[11] If a majority of your subconscious is on board with manifesting your new imagined outcome, you will likely have an easier time achieving it.

To understand how to transform beliefs, it may be helpful for you to first understand how beliefs are formed. You probably have particular views that you hold to be true about the world and a value system that developed during your upbringing from your parents and family members, other influential role models, or teachers. These can also be messages from society and culture, or a summation of all the experiences you have had in your life. You may believe that you are a clean slate when you are born or that someone else pre-selected part or all of your life before you were born. If you believe in reincarnation, depending on how many lives you lived previously, you may have established historical beliefs. This may impact your belief in your own free will, divine will, fate, or destiny.

It is also conceivable that you inherited some emotions or the pre-conditioning to hold certain beliefs, before birth in this lifetime. Life experiences may have changed genetic markers of the DNA of your ancestors, which then may be passed down to you.[12] For instance, research has shown that trauma creates DNA markers and that these markers can be passed to next generations, making it more difficult for them to cope with stress. However, since markers come and go, this is an adaptive evolutionary process that can be consciously altered by choosing a positive direction to create a legacy of positive conscious change. This is known as *resilience*—the ability to come out of a traumatic or a stressful experience changed in a positive manner.[13]

A combination of thoughts with emotions can form new beliefs. For example, if a young person sees what they interpret to be a friendly dog and they try to pet it—and it bites them, causing pain, bleeding, sadness, and anger—the person can develop a fear that dogs can cause pain and can't be trusted, even if they appear friendly. Positive beliefs can form the same way. If you take the same scenario, and the dog is friendly, likes being petted, and the person experiences pleasure, positive feelings could be associated with a friendly-looking dog.

Your beliefs may have formed in similar ways about "the other"— people, groups, organizations, and society. This may impact your ability to move something forward in your life that may involve relationships with these people, groups, organizations, or society.

Belief is so powerful it can impact your health and ability to heal. Many believe that health is wealth. This is especially true if you have experienced having some type of imbalance, illness, or disease of your mind or body that impacted your ability to carry out daily tasks and affected your overall sense of well-being and quality of life.

According to Wayne Jonas, MD, belief is so important that what you believe about your health and wellness may impact whether or not you are well. Jonas was the first Director for the Office of Alternative Medicine (now the National Center for Complementary and Integrative Health at the National Institutes of Health) and is the author of *How Healing Works*. He states that 80 percent or more of your healing, health, and wellness comes from within you— your beliefs, expectations, and what is meaningful to you.[14] This has been commonly referred to as *the placebo effect* or *the placebo response*, an often-misunderstood phenomenon that suggests there is real power in your belief that can help you heal or prevent disease.

The placebo response can occur when there is a belief or expectation that something positive will happen. For years it was primarily considered a low-number variable in research studies when the intervention being researched needed to be statistically more significant than the placebo response to be accepted as valid to treat or help the target condition. What has been happening for years is that science frequently ignored the person's power of belief and expectation as a valid way to create a positive outcome for healing to occur, to stay well, and to prevent disease.

The *nocebo response* is the opposite of the placebo response and can occur when there is a belief or expectation that something negative will happen. This may be associated with worry, fear, and negative emotions that keep you from the fulfilling life you would like to lead. Limiting or negative beliefs can hold you back. The good news is there are ways to elicit positive expectations and belief.

Researchers found that the placebo effect helped them discover how a person may heal. A person may assign a belief and meaning to a substance or intervention. Jonas and his colleague suggested that the placebo response be replaced by the words *meaning, context,* and *learning response,* or simply *the meaning response.* They redefined it as "the physiological, psychological, and clinical effects of meaning when a placebo (or inert treatment) is used."

Elements of your health and ability for deep healing are linked with your purpose in life. If you feel you have a purpose in life, especially one that gives back to others and is aligned with your values, research shows you will do better in all areas of your life. A life with meaning and purpose can prevent and treat chronic disease, reduce suffering, and prolong life.[15]

Herbert Benson, MD, who coined the term *the relaxation response,* found these same benefits to be true. When Benson was proposing that a person could alter their physiology—heart rate, blood pressure, and breath rate through mind-body practices, such as meditation—many of his colleagues dismissed his theory as simply the placebo response. So what did Dr. Benson do? He researched the placebo response. The placebo response has often been dismissed as "all in their heads." Benson found that the relaxation response was indeed the result of the mind affecting the body. Dr. Benson discovered that the placebo response was active more often than reported in research studies and found it had profound effects that went beyond a simple response in research studies.

Benson states in his book *Timeless Healing: The Power of Biology and Belief,* "I first began reviewing the scientific literature on the placebo effect in the mid-1970s, and shortly thereafter began publishing and speaking on its potential therapeutic benefits. Together with colleagues, I found that in the patient cases we reviewed, the effect I call *remembered wellness* was 70-90 percent effective, doubling and tripling the success rate that had always been attributed to the placebo effect."[10]

What Benson calls remembered wellness is the ability to harness the qualities of expectation and belief, and to remember the calm and confidence associated with health and happiness. He encourages people to develop a positive mental picture of the state of good health they want to achieve. This can be accessed more easily after eliciting the relaxation response. It is a form of mental or guided imagery similar to visualization practices used by athletes, for example, who imagine shooting a ball into a basket. The imagined practice can enhance performance and outcomes. (See page 72 to experience remembered wellness. Be sure to complete Phases 1 and 2 of the Benson-Henry Protocol for the full benefits.)

In my 2013 interview with Benson, he further said, "Belief and expectancy on the part of the patient; belief and expectancy on the part of the healthcare giver, the physician, the nurse, the therapist; and the belief and expectancy that's engendered by the relationship between the healthcare giver and the patient is vitally important, and so these often can lead to profound healings. For example, one study showed that people undergoing knee surgery—some had the actual surgery and others had simply an incision made without the surgery—but both believed the surgical approach was working. And those that had the incision that was only the incision, without the operation, often did as well as those who had the actual surgery, because there the belief and expectancy engendered the results. So you see that type of approach could be captured, that is belief and expectancy by what is pejoratively and erroneously called the placebo effect and believed the placebo effect." (The full article can be read here: https://holisticot.org/the-power-of-the-mind-in-healing-relaxation.)

Joe Dispenza, Doctor of Chiropractic, neuroscientist, and author summarizes this concept well in the simple title of his book: *You Are the Placebo: Making Your Mind Matter.*

> *Our deepest wounds integrated become our greatest strengths.*
> —Anna Freud

> *One does not become enlightened by imagining figures of light, but by making the darkness conscious.*
> —C. G. Jung

Transforming Beliefs and Expectations

Transforming your beliefs and expectations may be what is needed to manifest what you want. Some beliefs will be easy for you to transform on your own, through intuitive guidance or the exercises throughout this book. Others may be deeply ingrained, and you may have been practicing them consciously or unconsciously for years; these may take longer to be replaced with positive ones.

If it is difficult for you to believe that you can have what you want to manifest, you may need to heal emotions, negative thoughts, and grief-derived feelings. Work on building self-esteem and positive beliefs about yourself also helps neutralize thoughts and feelings holding you back, such as: "I don't deserve this," "That could never really happen to me," or "I won't feel safe."

Since most beliefs are just below the surface in the unconscious realm, it is helpful to access that part of you by using a relaxation response state. This can be done through professional help or alone by yourself.

Nicole Hoekstra-Voves, *Arctic Fox,* 2018

Here are some ways to change your beliefs into positive expectations and manifest your intentions. This is not an exhaustive list. Find what works for you.

Mindfulness

Practicing mindfulness meditation throughout your daily activities by observing your thoughts and beliefs, with no judgment and with love and compassion around your beliefs or what you want to manifest, may help to create new beliefs. By practicing mindfulness, you may be able to heal from past emotional wounds and transform thoughts and beliefs to new ones. By compassionately accepting your reaction to all of your experiences, you are more easily able to be an open channel for your intuition for new insights and beliefs to naturally form. You may then be able to step back and see your life from a nonjudging and more compassionate place. As you observe your thoughts, emotions, and body sensations, the tension may release in your mind and body. This may move you past resistance and connect you more deeply with your intuition, where new beliefs may form. (See mindfulness meditation on page 75.)

EFT

Emotional Freedom Technique (EFT) may help you transform beliefs as well as issues of self-confidence and self-esteem. EFT combines energy psychology and acupressure to alleviate physical, mental, emotional, and spiritual symptoms and reach positive goals. EFT is an efficacy-based practice according to the American Psychological Association. Several studies have shown statistical significance with lowering stress, physical and emotional pain, anxiety, depression, and post-traumatic stress syndrome. (See more in "Energy Healing Styles" section, page 94.)

According to the Association of Comprehensive Energy Psychology, energy psychology combines cognitive interventions (including focused awareness and mindfulness, imagined exposure to traumatic memories, positive outcomes, and cognitive reframing) simultaneously with the stimulation of one or more of the human bio-energy systems, such as meridians, chakras, and biofields.[16]

EFT is a relatively simple technique that can be taught to children and adults. The practitioner guides a client to focus on words, thoughts, and emotional or physical feelings in the body and energy system related to their problem or challenge. Simultaneously, acupressure is applied in the form of gentle touch or pressure, tapping on, or imagining touching fourteen major energy pathway points—the same found in acupuncture.

There are several leaders in the EFT field who have created trainings and education for healthcare professionals and lay people. Gary Craig coined the term "EFT" in 1995, and it quickly became popular as he shared it with the world via a free tutorial, workshops, and an introductory video series.

Craig developed EFT based on similar methods, such as Roger Callahan's Thought Field Therapy (TFT). TFT also uses tapping in a sequence in the form of a healing code, balancing the body's energy system to help eliminate most negative emotions within minutes, while promoting the body's own healing ability.

An EFT practitioner guides the client to select a challenging area of their life they would like to improve. They become aware of and notice what emotions they're feeling and where in their body they're experiencing them. The client can also select the opposite of what is distressing them—the positive of what they would like to experience or have happen in their life.

The classic process involves having a person rate their negative emotional or physical challenge on a scale from zero to ten, with ten the highest distress and zero when the problem is gone. They then tap while focusing on distressing thoughts or feelings while saying, "Even though I have (insert negative thought or feeling), I deeply and completely love and accept myself." When working with a child, for example, they might say, "Even though I have a tummy ache, I am still a good child."

Silvia Hartmann, PhD, founder of the Association of Meridian Therapies, has created several EFT training courses and has expanded the way EFT is practiced. She created the Heart and Soul method, in which the client first rates their area of focus on the Subjective Unit of Experience Scale (SUE).[17] This scale includes positive and negative feelings. The scale runs from -10 to 0 to 10+. Then the person places their hands over their heart center and repeats the words that are related to the challenge or positive outcome desired.

Both methods involve the person being guided in one to several rounds of action (tapping or touching) while repeating words or phrases that connect the client to a previously distressing experience or a positive experience they would like to move toward. The person is guided to focus on the physical body sensations, thoughts, and emotional feelings during the rounds. Often the person will experience a lowering of distressing thoughts, emotions, and physical symptoms, and new helpful insights with a higher rating on the SUE scale.

It is possible that everyone can benefit from EFT, as it has an ability to calm, relax, relieve emotional and physical pain, and bring harmony and flow to a disrupted energy system. EFT can help transform negative emotions and beliefs, and can assist with rewiring neural connections, improve immune system functioning, and enhance the healing of mind, body, and spirit. The mind and body are inseparable. EFT elicits the relaxation response, where intuition is more easily accessible.

You can use EFT for any stress-related problem, whether it manifests physically or mentally, from an emotion, or belief. As Gary Craig says, "Try it on everything." Sylvia Harman says, "We don't try to solve it, only evolve it." You may also find it interesting to use EFT to explore what you were taught or what you believe around issues such as money, family members, groups of people, organizations, nations, or anything you want to explore that you feel may be holding you back. Doing so, you can decrease energy-body stress and increase energy-body flow and increase positive expectations.

For example, do you believe money is good or bad, somewhere in between, or neutral? Do you believe money is easy or hard to get or keep? What do you believe having more money will bring you—a sense of security, freedom, pleasure? Do you believe it might bring you more problems? Explore all of your thoughts and beliefs. Complete a few EFT rounds until the stress has decreased and new intuitive thoughts and insights arise, replacing the old beliefs. What are your new beliefs?

If you believe you do not deserve what you long to manifest, it can be effective to bring the negative belief, emotion, or body sensation into an EFT session. You may be able to transform how you feel by pairing it with a positive statement that is all about loving and accepting yourself. For example, if you believe that you can't have your desired goal or have doubt about achieving it, your statement accompanying tapping could be, "Even though I doubt I can achieve my goal, I deeply and completely love and accept myself."

The best way to begin learning EFT is to experience it. It is highly recommended to be guided by a certified EFT practitioner for the best results and to have a session specifically tailored to you.

Here are a couple of EFT videos on YouTube that I created. The first one will help you transform or release negative beliefs, thoughts, and emotions. The second can help you positively reach your dreams and goals.

EFT for Negative Emotions and Thoughts: https://www.youtube.com/watch?v=HpYzBqzml_w&feature=youtu.be

Positive EFT – Reach Your Dreams and Goals: https://youtu.be/Ft25RC7ghww

Until you make the unconscious conscious, it will direct your life and you will call it fate.
–C. G. JUNG

Story

MaryAnn wanted more from her life. She had a successful job but would go home at night and spend most of her time alone watching TV. She wanted to engage in more activities but wasn't sure what they were. She wanted more friends but had a fear of being rejected and was suffering with social anxiety.

She came for an appointment and it was clear that MaryAnn was suffering from lack of self-love and self-acceptance, often known as low self-esteem. She completed a self-esteem inventory, and it showed that she had moderately low self-esteem. I taught her relaxation techniques, mindfulness meditation, and EFT that she learned to practice in between her sessions with me.

She wanted to meet more friends but didn't know how to go about it. She felt that no one would like her or find her interesting, based on past experiences in conversations with people. They would generally only listen to her briefly and then start talking to someone else.

I encouraged her to pick one or two activities that she enjoyed doing or something new she wanted to explore. I suggested that would introduce her to places where she might meet people with similar interests.

I helped her process feelings of fear of rejection with EFT and mindfulness, and she learned to listen to her intuition in meditation and through use of her own intuitive card deck. Along with me, she also read the book, *Self-Esteem*, by Matthew McKay and Patrick Fanning; we read one chapter at a time, in between our sessions. She also completed the exercises, and we discussed what she learned and any new intuitive insights. She learned how much her lack of relationship with her parents growing up impacted her ability to regard herself with warmth and love and feel her value, worth, and right to have positive experiences.

She completed an inventory on what leisure activities she enjoyed doing the most. She loved birdwatching but hadn't done it in years. She wanted to get back into it, as well as dancing. After a few months, she felt ready and signed up for a weekend birdwatching retreat and began taking dance classes. She met new friends on the retreat and now goes birdwatching regularly. She has met a group of new friends where she dances, feels loved and accepted by them, and meets them socially.

After several months of every-other-week appointments with me, I asked her to take the self-esteem inventory again; it increased to fairly good self-esteem. She is now having a great time with her friends. She says she has learned to like herself and is working toward loving herself.

Unintended Outcomes

There may be times when, no matter your best efforts, what you intend to achieve hasn't come into fruition the way that you had planned. When something isn't going right, there may be a higher purpose at play, more action may need to be taken, the timing needs to be right, or your conditioned beliefs, thoughts, or emotions may have gotten in your way.

Maybe you were not listening fully to all of your intuition, and you need to spend more time fully listening. Or it's possible that you were listening, yet the outcome may actually be what your intuition had in mind as another, better path for you. In other words, what you thought you wanted was not really in alignment with *what is really good for you*.

Story

Carmen wanted her relationship to work. She loved the person she was dating, but her partner wasn't making a commitment. Carmen had been meditating for over a year and had made her own intuitive card deck. She consulted her intuitive cards to give her insight into the relationship.

She pulled cards in a three-card spread for past, present, and future. The first card was an image of a person, the second card was a house, and the third, or outcome card, was distance with a long arrow pointing forward. At the time, she interpreted that the cards were showing her that she was meant to be single and to move toward her goal of buying a house on her own. She thought that the arrow meant to move on from the relationship. Since the relationship was struggling, she and her partner broke up.

Within the next couple of years, she accomplished more of her dreams with a good job and bought her own house. She focused on personal and spiritual development in her life. Then, out of the blue, the previous relationship rekindled when her partner contacted her by email, sharing how empty his life was without her. They began dating again and got married a few years later.

She thought back to when she'd consulted her cards about the relationship, and in hindsight she had a new interpretation. Maybe in addition to the first interpretation to be single and to buy her own house, the relationship would be revisited in the future. Carmen and her husband now live together in the house she bought. The relationship has grown and is now more mature and healthy for both of them, since she was able to achieve goals and grow on her own. They have been married for ten years and grow more devoted to each other every day.

The late poet and singer Leonard Cohen, who practiced Buddhism for most of his adult life, once said words to the effect: When you don't get what you believe you should get, maybe what you needed to experience is *not getting* what you believed you should get.

Despite your efforts to be safe, there are hurricanes, floods, fires, earthquakes, volcanoes, or tornadoes. War, violence, guns, abuse, neglect, homelessness, and famine are sadly and tragically experienced daily by millions around the world. Political choices are made that may seem beyond your control. You or someone you love may experience an illness or be born with a congenital disease or have a terminal illness. There are accidents we may not fully recover from. And we will most definitely die or transition from this earth, even if you or a loved one wants to live longer or have an improved quality of life.

If there are insurmountable obstacles on your path, there may be something you need to learn, or there may be powerful forces at play that are simply beyond your ability to believe. Despite all of these challenges, no matter what the outcome, you can still listen to your intuition and learn how you can make a positive impact in the world. If enough people do this, there may be a tipping point toward more positive outcomes for everyone. So continuing toward your desired goals may help transform individual as well as collective opposition.

Your intuition may guide you in making healthcare decisions or coping with grief. Your intuition may help you come to more peace and acceptance, allowing you to experience your emotions in a mindful way—with love and acceptance. Maybe your challenges will teach you humility, grace, love, wisdom, or other life lessons.

Story

Bill was sad that his dad was diagnosed with Alzheimer's disease. He had been witnessing his dad's memory slip for a few years, and now his father needed twenty-four-hour care. Bill described his relationship with his dad as mediocre, but he loved his dad and was dutiful and responsible.

He provided the care his dad needed in his own home for as long as he could, but finances were becoming exhausted as the care needs were increasing, and he needed to move him into a skilled nursing facility. Even though Bill felt he had an okay relationship with his dad, underneath he had been angry for years. As a child he sometimes felt neglected, and his dad would at times drink heavily, get angry at him, and even physically abuse him.

Bill's emotions were coming more to the surface with all the extra stress of caring for his father. During the time of his memory slipping, his dad became more and more physically and emotionally vulnerable. Bill felt his heart opening more to his dad but was still angry and resentful.

Bill practiced t'ai chi, went for a daily walk or jog, and listened to inner wisdom guided imagery a few times a week. He was guided by his intuition to forgive his father. He had also recently been hearing family members share stories about how his grandfather died young, when Bill's dad was only nine years old. Consequently, his grandmother had to work harder and longer hours, leaving his dad alone or cared for by his siblings.

Bill was guided in several EFT sessions by me, and he learned mindfulness meditation. This helped him to process his feelings of grief and more easily connect to his own heart and intuition. When his father's disease progressed to the point where he could no longer verbally communicate, Bill said to his father, "I forgive you," and imagined his father saying he was sorry and how much he loved him. Bill established a new relationship with his dad where he felt love for and from his dad. He developed a spiritual relationship with his dad.

When his dad died, Bill was sad but was grateful for the new relationship that they had formed. Bill believed he could communicate with his dad, whenever he wanted, through his intuition. He felt more love from his dad than ever before. Bill was more peaceful and satisfied and is enjoying his life more than he ever had been able to before.

Destiny or Free Will

How much destiny or free will is at play in your life? That is an age-old question. You may believe everything is predetermined or created by a higher power, or that karma from a previous life is with you in this one, and that there are no mistakes. Or you may believe everything that happens is entirely of your making. Ultimately, what you believe is up to you.

Your will may be the most powerful form of energy you have to create what you want in your life. The statement, "I *will* . . ." can gather your intention, focus, and energy in the direction of what you want to make happen. How many times throughout the day are you saying to yourself: "I *will* do this," "I *will* go there," or "I *will* eat this"? Your will may determine what it is you will manifest and what you will not.

You may believe that you are meant to be here to have certain life experiences. It's possible there are certain life experiences or lessons you are meant to learn in this lifetime. Perhaps your will is what chooses to have certain experiences in order to learn, grow, give, or share, and determine how much love you will receive.

Your purpose for being alive may be to share gifts that are unique to you. You have certain gifts that your soul is likely trying to get you to listen to, in order to serve the world. There may be this plan for you, and if you're listening fully to your intuition you should be able to align with it.

According to astrology, you have a personal *purpose* — your sun sign and house it is located in on your chart. You also have a *mission*—where 12:00 noon was on the day you were born, known as the *medium coeli* (Latin for *middle of the heavens*) or MC, indicating your outer mission and how you may serve humanity or society.[18, 19, 20] You can look at your astrological chart on websites, such as Astro.com, where you can enter your birth place, date, and time to see your own birth or natal chart. It's always better to schedule time with someone trained in astrology to help you get clear on your mission or purpose, but you can study the fascinating subject yourself.

Even if you don't look to astrology, you can look inside and find the clues. Or perhaps you know your purpose or mission, and you just need to focus on how best to manifest it.

We but mirror the world. All the tendencies present in the outer world are to be found in the world of our body. If we could change ourselves, the tendencies in the world would also change. As a man changes his own nature, so does the attitude of the world change towards him. This is the divine mystery supreme. A wonderful thing it is, and the source of our happiness. We need not wait to see what others do.
  —MAHATMA GANDHI

Time

Much of what happens in life may be about timing. What you think you want, that which seems in alignment with your intuition, may come to fruition in the right timing. Sometimes our intuition will lead us in a certain direction for us to have certain experiences at certain times. We learn with every experience and adjust for new endeavors.

This is why we have seasons in nature. You have your own internal seasons and timing. There is a time to plan your garden. A time to plant seeds and water. There is a time to weed the garden and help it grow. There is a time to enjoy watching the flowers and see your garden come to fruition. There is a time to harvest and enjoy the bounty of your efforts.

Ecclesiastes 3:1-8[21]

–Anonymous

To every thing there is a season,

and a time to every purpose under the heaven:

A time to be born, a time to die;

A time to plant, and a time to pluck up that which is planted;

A time to kill, and a time to heal;

A time to break down, and a time to build up;

A time to weep, and a time to laugh;

A time to mourn, and a time to dance;

A time to cast away stones, and a time to gather stones together;

A time to embrace, and a time to refrain from embracing;

A time to get, and a time to lose;

A time to keep, and a time to cast away;

A time to rend, and a time to sew;

A time to keep silence, and a time to speak;

A time to love, and a time to hate;

A time of war, and a time of peace.

Story

Early in my career, after I took a break from occupational therapy, I had my own massage therapy and reflexology practice. For a few years I saw how it helped people lower stress, pain, anxiety, depression, and insomnia, and I really wanted to bring these healing tools to mainstream healthcare at a hospital.

I have lived in St. Paul, Minnesota, most of my life, and I envisioned that I would provide massage therapy at a hospital located in St. Paul. I thought how rewarding it would be to research these approaches for various populations and show how beneficial they can be.

For several years I envisioned myself providing care to people who were suffering in hospitals and clinics, where sometimes pharmaceutical medications only marginally helped or did not help at all. I felt how good it would be for them to experience this deep relaxation, being more pain free, with less stress, improved ability to function, and feeling more happy and free. I felt how good I would feel being able to help them and have fewer people suffering in the world. But still, no mainstream job manifested.

A few years after I'd been stymied getting a job in the St. Paul hospital, I learned that the program was closing and that a new one was opening in Minneapolis at Abbott Northwestern Hospital. Had I gotten a job at the St. Paul hospital it would have quickly gone away. Instead, more intention by many people needed to align for the program to be successful from the grassroots all the way up to management and the executive leadership team.

I became a part of the amazing Integrative Medicine team, where I was able to work with people at their hospital bedsides and at the new outpatient center, The Penny George Institute for Health and Healing. We were so successful in reducing pain, stress, and anxiety levels that a research study was conducted that demonstrated the statistically significant efficacy of many approaches, such as massage therapy, meditation, guided imagery, energy healing, and music therapy. The program continues to serve many people who have been able to experience the benefits of integrative healthcare.

Acceptance of Now

As you saw earlier, there is evidence that taking time to appreciate what you have and what you would like to achieve can increase the positivity about how you feel in your life, and therefore improve your energy and attract what you want. These two seemingly polar opposites can coexist and enhance one another—*appreciating the now, while working toward the future.*

If you're overly focused on manifesting something for the future, you may miss the good that is happening now. You may later find yourself wistfully looking back at this time in your life, wishing you had taken the time to appreciate and enjoy all that was good. You may find it's easier to think about the next thing, or that "life will be better when x, y, z happens," because you may feel like you are going through a hard time. We are conditioned to think that happiness is off in the future. While this may be true for some situations, your life is happening now, and you can learn to switch into more positive states.

Focus on what's positive, going well, and what you are grateful for, while intending to manifest a desired goal. Discover what's not working and how you may be able to improve it. Practice acceptance of now—including your acceptance of your reactions to what is happening now—while working toward what you want while trying to be present. This is the essence of mindfulness.

While you are working toward your goals, you can simultaneously be grateful for the ability to see, walk, enjoy a cup of tea, laugh at a funny joke, and feel the awe of nature. You may come to see that your life is more okay than you may have realized, and you just needed to transform limiting beliefs and emotions around past negative or even traumatic experiences.

Perhaps, all that was really upsetting you was your internal state versus an external one. As you practice more appreciation and acceptance of now, along with manifesting your intentions, notice how different you feel and what may change for the better in your life.

Written Exercise

- What beliefs that you hold true are serving you in your life?
- What beliefs that you hold true may be limiting you in your life?
- How can you transform your beliefs in alignment to what you want to create or manifest in your life (hint: begin with intention)?

Experiential

Set an intention to explore or transform a limiting belief. Become aware of or write down all of your thoughts, beliefs, emotions, and body sensations associated with this belief. After meditation, become aware of or write down all of your new thoughts.

Listen to the Mindfulness Meditation – Loving Yourself:
https://youtu.be/9osXogDGCnY

After the meditation, become aware of any new thoughts, beliefs, emotions, and body sensations associated with this belief. What has changed? Have new insights come to you? Take note of this or write it in your journal.

11. Spirituality and Intuition

We are not human beings having a spiritual experience.
We are spiritual beings having a human experience.
–Pierre Teilhard de Chardin (authorship disputed)

As we've discussed previously, spirituality and intuition often go hand in hand. Intuition may be your divine connection to your spirituality, help to strengthen it, or be synonymous with it—source, higher power, higher self, soul, God, the one, or whatever term you find meaningful. Cultivating your intuition regularly may help you experience being connected to something greater than yourself and living with more meaning and purpose.

By quieting and listening within, you can connect to the peaceful and joyful place within—your loving, compassionate, and wise self—and experience the divine. As you feel connected, separateness will evaporate and your spiritual life develops further. You will likely feel more grounded and peaceful. You will likely then be able to have a personal relationship with your God or higher power, without an intermediary. You may or may not follow any spiritual or religious practice. It is not necessary for you to consider your intuitive development supportive of your spiritual practice, but for many this is the case.

For centuries, spiritual leaders, poets, and mystics have known that activities that help quiet the mind, such as meditation and prayer, can create an ineffable sense of oneness and peace that is often associated with spirituality and religious practices. Even if you've never considered yourself a spiritual person you may have experiences that you may consider to be in this realm.

The word "spirit" comes from the Latin root word *spiritus*, which means breath, wind, air, soul, or psyche.[1] Spirit is generally considered metaphysical—that which is transcendent or a reality beyond what is perceptible to the senses. You may experience your spirit as your unique self, consciousness, or energy; it is foundational to who you are. It is part of the mind-body-spirit connection and includes what drives you or gives you meaning or purpose.

Do you believe in a God or higher power, angels, or that prayer works? If you do, you have a lot of company. According to a few polls, 90 percent of Americans believe in God, 77 percent of adult Americans believe in angels, and 90 percent have prayed for healing.[2,3,4] If you do not believe in such things, connecting with your intuition may support development of your own unique beliefs that can sustain you in life.

Spirituality may be as unique and individual as each person having a spiritual experience. Spirituality may be understood as "the personal quest for understanding answers to ultimate questions about life, about meaning, and about relationship with the sacred or transcendent, which may (or may not) lead to or arise from the development of religious rituals and the formation of community."[5] What does spirituality mean to you?

The process of engaging with your intuition through the various exercises in this book or in whatever way is meaningful for you may become a spiritual practice, enhance the one you already have, or help develop it. Your intuition will help your spirituality and engender answers to many questions—including big ones such as:

Why am I here?
What's meaningful to me?
What matters to me or gives me purpose?

Seven Spiritual Hungers

Spirituality is essential to us as human beings. Howard Clinebell, PhD, found over his thirty-plus years of psychological counseling and pastoral care, that there are seven spiritual hungers that humans have in common. The hunger to:

1. Experience healing and empowerment of love—from others, self, and ultimate source.
2. Experience renewing times of transcendence—expansive moments beyond the immediate sensory spheres.
3. Have vital beliefs that lend meaning and hope in the midst of losses, tragedies, and failures.
4. Have values, priorities, and life commitments centered in issues of justice, integrity, and love to provide guidance in personally and socially responsible living.
5. Discover inner wisdom, creativity, and love of self—and unique transpersonal/spiritual self.
6. Develop a deepening awareness of our oneness with other people, the natural world, and all living things.
7. Have spiritual resources to help heal grief, guilt, resentment, unforgiveness, self-rejection, and shame, and deepen experiences of trust, self-esteem, hope, joy, and love of life.[6,7]

What *spiritual hungers* grab you and want your attention? Are there any of these that you wish to explore? Deepening your intuition may help you enhance these aspects of your spiritual life.

Ways to Get in Touch with or Enhance Your Spirituality

There are countless ways to get more in touch with and enhance your spirituality. What intuitively is calling you? All of the aforementioned tips, suggestions, and exercises in this book may help you.

Are there any spiritual or religious paths you are curious about? Any that you used to practice you would like to revisit? If you have a spiritual or religious practice already, perhaps you may like to spend more time with it. Do you feel you need a new spiritual or religious interest path? Consider exploring more.

What other activities can you think of to connect with your spirituality? The activities you come up with and the ones below will draw you closer to yourself and something greater. Take time to connect with what gives you meaning and purpose and inspires you, and find ways to participate in that. Listen to your intuition about which activities will support you and follow them.

- Meditate
- Pray
- Contemplate
- Practice intention
- Strengthen positive beliefs and transform negative beliefs
- Read spiritual books, articles, poems, or inspirational messages
- Be in nature
- Spend time with art, music, or creativity
- Visit peaceful, sacred, serene, or holy places
- Go to a church, temple, synagogue, gurdwara, mosque, or other place of worship
- Participate in a spiritual community
- Take spiritual workshops or go on a retreat
- Take spiritual classes, such as meditation, relaxation, guided imagery, spiritual development, intuitive development, energy healing, or yoga
- Cleanse your space with sage, essential oils, music, prayer, or your intention
- Light a candle
- Go for a walk
- Sing, play, or listen to music
- Move your body or exercise in ways that help you be in the flow, the moment, or practice mindfulness
- Dance
- Yoga
- T'ai chi

- Play full-body games or sports
- Engage in aerobic activities like jogging or running
- Laugh, watch a comedy
- Cry
- Spend time with loved ones—family or friends
- Make new friends
- Spend time with animals
- Create your own altar with meaningful objects
- Create sacred space
- Create meaningful spiritual practices, habits, or routines
- Participate in an activity or ritual with the intention to draw into your life what you want, or let go of what you want to release
- Create space to release any unresolved grief you may have
- Forgive yourself, forgive others
- Open to possibilities and joyful positive expectation of what you want to create in your life
- Practice gratitude—find at least three things to be grateful for each day and feel how good this feels
- Participate in activities or rituals meaningful to you
- Engage in meaningful spiritual or philosophical conversations that stimulate your own spiritual unfolding
- Visit or plant a garden
- Take care of the earth
- Follow what inspires you
- Be gentle, loving, and kind with yourself
- Love yourself more, love others more
- Just be

Spiritual Gifts

You come to this planet with certain interests and strengths that show you your inherent special gifts. They have been endowed to you to help you in your life and enhance the lives of others—your family and friends and acquaintances—through art, communication, healing, compassion and understanding, education, entertainment, or whatever draws you.

The world is in dire need of your gifts. You may have already followed your natural interests, or maybe you're not entirely sure what they are. Your intuition can help you get more clarity on what these gifts are and develop them by engaging in regular intuitive practices, such as the ones outlined in this book. Your intuition can continue to guide you in how you share these gifts, with whom, and where.

Gifts of the spirit are described in the Bible in Corinthians 12. Whether you're Christian or not, this passage describes them well. They are likely mentioned in a similar fashion through various religious or spiritual practices. The quotation says:

> There are different kinds of gifts, but the same
> Spirit. There are different kinds of service, but the
> same Lord. There are different kinds of working,
> but the same God works all of them in all men.
>
> Now to each one the manifestation of the Spirit is given
> for the common good. To one there is given through the
> Spirit the message of wisdom, to another the message
> of knowledge by means of the same Spirit, to another
> faith by the same Spirit, to another gifts of healing by
> that one Spirit, to another miraculous powers, to an-
> other prophecy, to another distinguishing between spir-
> its, to another speaking in different kinds of tongues,
> and to still another the interpretation of tongues. All
> these are the work of one and the same Spirit, and
> he gives them to each one, just as he determines.[8]

Oracles, Prophets, and Mystics

Throughout the ages there have been prophets, mystics, and oracles who have displayed various gifts of the spirit. They have received and then shared spiritual messages and visions from divine sources, such as angels, gods, a higher source, wise spiritual beings, or from those who were once incarnate. Their messages have been kept alive over centuries by many who feel they provide truth, inspiration, beauty, comfort, or solace. Religious and spiritual practices are often built on these messages. Prophet, mystic, and oracle seem to have similar definitions.

A prophet may be thought of as a spiritual seer, one who utters divinely inspired revelations or is regarded by a group of followers as the final authoritative revealer of God's will (such as Muhammad, the *Prophet* of Allah). A prophet is gifted with more than ordinary spiritual and moral insight. They are an inspirational poet who foretells future events with spiritual truths.[9]

A prophet is someone who is naturally gifted and has usually worked hard to understand their gift. They have often experienced and overcome great challenges that have brought them to the depths of their soul, looking for answers.[10] This yearning or quest may have opened them to receive. Their consciousness may have been ready to receive the messages and, with humility, bring the messages to humanity.

A mystic is a person who attains insight into mysteries transcending ordinary human knowledge by direct communication with the divine or immediate intuition while in a state of spiritual ecstasy. A mystic may or may not have been initiated into religious mysteries involving or characterized by esoteric, otherworldly, or symbolic practices or content, such as certain religious ceremonies and art, or spiritually significant or ethereal connections.[11]

Mysticism and quiet contemplation are common to all of us, according to Karen Armstrong, author of texts on religious topics, a former Roman Catholic nun, and one of the foremost British commentators on religious affairs.[12] In her book, *A History of God: The 4,000-Year Quest of Judaism, Christianity and Islam*, she states:

> The mystical experience of God has certain characteristics that are common to all faiths. It is a subjective experience that involves an interior journey, not a perception of an objective fact outside the self: it is undertaken through the image-making part of the mind—often called the imagination—rather than through the more cerebral, logical faculty. Finally, it is something that the mystic creates in himself or herself deliberately: certain physical or mental exercises yield the final version; it does not always come upon them unawares.[12]

Similar to or the same as a mystic or prophet is an oracle. An oracle may be a priest or priestess who is a medium or conduit between this world and another, or a messenger through whom advice or prophecy was sought from a deity or the gods in classical antiquity, such as in the Oracle of Delphi.[13] Delphi was a significant ancient-Greek religious sanctuary considered sacred by the God Apollo, or God of the Sun. The sanctuary, located near the Gulf of Corinth on Mt. Parnassus, was thought to be the center of the world and the home to the famous oracle of Apollo who provided enigmatic predictions and guidance to city-states and individuals. Delphi is now considered a cultural treasure and is listed as a world heritage site by UNESCO—United Nations Educational, Scientific and Cultural Organization.[14,15] On the Temple of Apollo of Delphi is inscribed: "Know thyself."

In addition to an oracle being a person, an oracle can be a divinatory tool, such as the tarot, *I Ching*, runes, numerology, or any other tool that helps you focus and receive to help you "divine" answers for insight and guidance. Your intuitive cards can serve you this way. (See page 121.)

Science will, in all probability, be increasingly
impregnated by mysticism.
–Pierre Teilhard de Chardin

Be Your Own Prophet

Throughout this book, you have been learning how to connect to a higher vibration, develop your gifts, and receive guidance to improve your life and others' lives. With practice and the tools provided, you will discover more consistent confidence with your intuition so that you can be your own prophet, mystic, and oracle.

While you are developing and learning to trust your intuitive abilities, it may be best to find a teacher or someone with experience in this topic—someone who has already developed their intuition who can assist and validate your intuitive insights and experiences. Or you may find inspiration from someone you already know, who you deem to be a prophet.

Who are your favorite prophets and why? I asked this question to a group of people and got a variety of responses. The responses show that it seems that anybody from history or modern times can be considered a prophet. They are all around us—and inside of us.

Here is a list of people's choices.[16] Are there any you would add? As you read through this list, you will find many outside of what is considered religion, who will perhaps inspire you.

Jesus, St. John the Baptist, Mary mother of Jesus, St. Faustina, St. Teresa of Calcutta, St. Gianna Molla, and many more! The reason for all of the above is because they have inspired me and how to live my life serving others and loving God.

Matthew 10: 40-42:

He who receives you received Me, and he who receives Me received Him who sent Me. He who receives a prophet because he is a prophet shall receive a prophet's reward. . . . And whoever gives to one of these little ones even a cup of cold water because he is a disciple, truly, I say to you he shall not lose his reward.

Rumi, Kabir, Mother Teresa, St. John of the Cross, Black Elk, Swami Satchidananda, Yogananda, Thomas Aquinas, Lao Tzu, Mencius

The songs of Solomon and David in the Bible

The Sophia Dragon Tribe—they include many of the well-known female masters—but it is about your own self-empowerment, with them as mentors.

People I like who have not been mentioned yet: St. Francis of Assisi, St. Teresa of Ávila, Deepak Chopra, and Marianne Williamson. You might also like to read Lissa Rankin's work on the mind/body healing connection.

Alexandria Ocasio-Córtez and Edward Ka-Spel

Mr. Rogers

Dalai Lama

Thich Nhat Hanh

Adyashanti—modern-day teacher of Truth

Kahlil Gibran, both Johns, and I especially liked The Prophet.

Muad'Dib

As an educator, I'm inspired by Maria Montessori. She had a re-markable and ahead-of-her-time understanding of infant, child, ad-olescent, and adult development. Instead of a blank slate that must be filled by their teachers, young people have their own self that needs opportunities to come alive. Thus, "follow the child."

I have read many of the above-named writers, thinkers, and proph-ets. The one I might remember best is Larry Mondello. He was Beaver Cleaver's best friend on *Leave It to Beaver*. In one episode, Beaver had caused his parents a lot of drama and grief, and he sweat-ed mightily over what would happen as a consequence. Although I couldn't have been more than five or six years old, I have always remembered what his friend told him to calm him down. He said, "Heck, Beave, relax, life isn't as hard as you're making it, it just hap-pens to you!" This has proven to be excellent counsel for sixty years now! Funny but true!

Dr. Joe Dispenza, *Breaking the Habit of Being Yourself: How to Lose Your Mind and Create a New One*; also *Becoming Supernatural*. Some fantastic chakra and energy meditations!

Helena Blavatsky, Annie Besant, Carlos Castañeda, Jack Parsons, Remedíos Varo

Ron Smothermon: *Winning Through Enlightenment*. He wrote sim-ply and directly, and I could feel his love for the reader in every page.

I am influenced by *I and Thou* and Martin Buber's philosophy about relationships and communication. When I have interactions with people I don't know, for example a clerk or a server, I try to make eye contact, recognize them as an individual with a life be-yond this meeting, and interact with them in a person-to-person rather than strictly transactional manner, so as to make all human encounters authentic.

Scott Hahn

Jeff Cavins and Sri

Several in the Bible. John the Baptist was considered to be a prophet and friend of Jesus when he walked the earth as a man. There are many in the word of God. Bible is a road map for healthy life relationships. Teaches all about that. That all God's ways are a relationship with Him and others.

James Dobson on relationships. Jack Canfield, the author of *Chicken Soup for the Soul.*

Paulo Coelho

Spiritual Healing

Longevity research from Stanford and Duke universities shows that, "The number-one predictor for longevity, good health, and happiness for both men and women across cultures is having a strong spiritual base."[17]

Spirituality has been identified as playing a significant role in healing, disease prevention, and wellness. However, in everyday life, when we are engaging in healthy lifestyles and promoting better self-care, spirituality is not always addressed. Yet it is inextricably linked to lifestyle, behaviors, and environment. As discussed earlier, spiritual or religious practices, such as prayer or meditation, can lead to better health outcomes, including increased energy, longer lifespan, better coping skills, and overall quality of life during an illness. Research indicates that there is a strong relationship between the degree to which healthcare practitioners address emotional and spiritual needs and overall patient satisfaction.[18]

As you have read throughout this book, you have learned that quieting the mind through various activities, such as meditation and inducing the relaxation response is vital for connecting to your intuition, health, and well-being. What is fascinating is that people who have elicited the relaxation response have also reported experiencing a connection with something greater than them, and they feel a more spiritual connection. In addition, research has shown that when this occurs, people can experience fewer medical symptoms.[19]

Belief in something greater than you has also been correlated with better health outcomes. Herbert Benson, MD, found that people who experienced increased spirituality from the relaxation response described two aspects of the experience: (1) the presence of an energy, a force, a power—God—that was beyond themselves; and (2) this presence felt close to them. The people who felt a presence had the greatest health benefits.

Jared D. Kass and Herbert Benson's studies "found that those who elicit the relaxation response regularly for more than one month had higher spirituality scores than those who did so less than one month. It didn't matter if you were novice or an old-timer, religious or nonreligious; the effects and rewards of the faith factor proved possible for very diverse individuals."[19]

The Faith Factor

Faith or belief opens you to positive expectations that can help with health and wellness. Once you experience spiritual connection, your faith in it will naturally evolve. A combination of intention and positive expectation may be at play in health and wellness. So becoming clearer with your intuition and dissolving negativity may help with positive intention and expectation.

Spiritual and religious practices usually promote healthy behaviors. Conditions that have been helped by religious belief include, but are not limited to:[19]

- Reduced alcohol consumption
- Reduced nicotine use
- Reduced drug use
- Improved psychological symptoms, including adjustment and coping

- Reduced depression
- Reduced hostility
- Reduced anxiety
- Improved general health
- Reduced blood pressure
- Improved quality of life in cancer patients
- Improved quality of life in heart disease patients
- Increased survival

During times of emotional stress, change, physical illness, or death, you may find yourself re-evaluating your connection to a creator, God, or higher power. Perhaps you suffer doubt or fear. You or a loved one may be struggling with questions, such as:

Why am I sick?
What's the purpose or meaning of my pain and suffering?
Will I live or die?

You or your loved one may find it helpful to consider:[18]

- What are my sources of hope, strength, comfort, or peace?
- What are my spiritual beliefs or religious practices?
- Am I part of a religious or spiritual community?
- What spiritual practices do I find most helpful personally?
- Do I meditate or pray?
- What gives me meaning or purpose in life?
- What activities can help me connect to my spirituality, faith, and positive belief?

Soul Connection

The light within—your inner self, true self, or the soul—is known as the *Atman* in Sanskrit. Atman is the essence of you that is beyond identification with phenomena and the false ego, which is considered not to be your true intuitive and loving self. Through the lens of Hindu philosophy, the *Atman* is the same as the transcendent self or *Brahman*,[20] with Brahman being the highest universal principle, or the ultimate reality in the universe. It is pervasive, permanent, genderless, infinite, and the source of eternal truth and bliss. It does not change and at the same time is the cause of all changes.

Metaphysically, Brahman is a binding unity behind the diversity within everything that exists in the universe. Brahman and the Atman are identical; it is inside you and each living being, and it can be found everywhere with a connected spiritual oneness in all that exists.[21] Brahman is a key concept described as the *Cosmic Principle* in the Vedas (*veda*, meaning "knowledge"), which are religious texts from ancient India that contain the oldest Sanskrit literature and scriptures of Hinduism. Brahman is extensively discussed in the early *Upanishads*, which are texts about meditation, philosophy, and spiritual knowledge.[22] In the *Upanishads*, Brahman has been described in a variety of ways as *Sat-cit-ānanda*—truth-consciousness-bliss. This is what you will experience when you are connected with your intuition.

Self-Liberation

When you find the light within and attain self-knowledge through experiencing your true self (Atman) as the same as the Brahman, then you can attain liberation or *moksha*. Being in an intuitive state of consciousness can help you do this. When you are connected to your intuition, feeling with your senses, you will feel your Atman and Brahman as one. It is a beautiful state of being that will keep you wanting to return to it again and again, feel it more often, and function from it—ultimately living each moment in this exquisite state. This may be thought of as to "Align with the Divine" (a phrase that came to me one day).

Spiritual Communication

While being with your intuition, you may experience connection to wise beings, angels, messengers, passed loved ones, animals, or other spirits that communicate with you. Your loved ones who have died or passed on may only be a thought away.

You can use your intuition to communicate with passed loved ones. Simply imagining they are there with you can enhance your connection.

You can use the inner wisdom guided imagery this way, and imagine that the wise being is your loved one (see page 88). While you increase your own intuitive abilities and confidence, you can also seek out a professional intuitive or medium who can connect in a meditative, focused state with the spirit world and assist you to communicate with passed loved ones. This may or may not resolve grief, but may help ease it.

Rebecca Austill-Clausen, OTR/L, is an occupational therapist who had a spiritually transformative experience of spontaneously communicating with her brother after his death. She learned how to communicate with her brother at her own will. This experience led to her personal healing and development of spiritual and healing skills, allowing her to live a more meaningful, happy, and healthy life. She shares her story in her book *Change Maker: How My Brother's Death Woke Up My Life*. You can watch or listen to an interview, "Healing with Spiritual Communication and Reiki," with her here: https://youtu.be/rHdlG16au_k

Near-Death Experiences

I think the most important thing I've learned in my studies is that whatever we happen to be chasing in life, whether knowledge or power or fame or whatever, the most important thing we can do while we're alive is to learn how to love.
—RAYMOND MOODY, MD, RESEARCHER
OF NEAR-DEATH EXPERIENCES[24]

Raymond Moody, MD, coined the term *near-death experience* based on his patients' similar stories about being clinically dead and then coming back to life. The similar features that people tend to describe are being out of their physical body and seeing people around them, but being unable to communicate with them. Many will experience a tube or tunnel of light often described as the most peaceful, serene, comforting, and loving feeling they have ever experienced. Of the stories he has gathered, this light often asks them two questions related to: (1) "What did you learn?"; and (2) "How did you love?" They often describe wanting to go toward this light, but something brings them back. These people often have a change of outlook on life, with increased meaning and purpose for living. Dr. Moody has spent a lifetime gathering stories and studying this phenomenon. He is sure that life continues after death.[23]

There is a convincing story of a spiritual afterlife by Eben Alexander, MD, who shares his experiences of visiting heaven in his book *Proof of Heaven*. Dr. Alexander is a neurosurgeon who contracted bacterial meningitis and was in a coma for seven days. He describes himself as not having been a particularly religious person, although he would attend church on Sundays with his family. He shares his belief that he experienced heaven during a coma, where any form of consciousness should not have been possible—and he would know because he's a neurosurgeon. He had experiences that gave him meaningful and accurate information about an important person in his life—things he had not previously known. He came back with a new understanding that love is what matters most, and that we are all more powerful than we often think we are. He is working to gain acceptance in the sciences of medicine and physics and is making inroads.

Story

Naomi's mother had just passed, due to an aggressive form of cancer. Fortunately, Naomi had been able to spend much of the last few months of her mother's life with her, and they had many conversations. Her mother expressed that she wanted to be cremated and have her ashes contained in an antique blue canning jar, which she had chosen for her burial vessel. She told her family to add pretty stones to the jar before it was buried. After her mother died, Naomi examined stones while gardening and on walks, mentally checking in with her mom and asking if each was what she wanted. The reply was always the same: "It's nice, but no, not that one."

Naomi had a collection of amethysts in her dining room, and when she would walk past the geodes, she would sense her mom's energy and felt that her mom wanted an amethyst. For days she repeatedly received the same message, but she felt that they were too large. Her mother's energy was persistently present whenever she was close to the purple

Naomi's crystal: *above*, one piece; *below*, two pieces

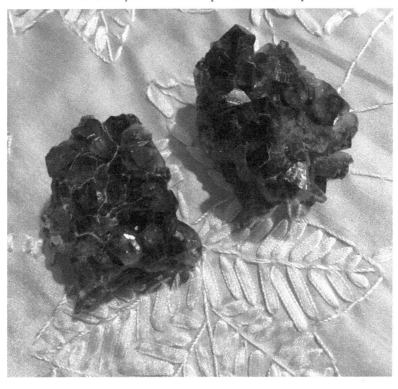

stones, so she conceded to give them more consideration. She handled each one, asking her mother which one she wanted. She continued to argue with her mother that the stone would be too large to fit in the jar. As she held the geode that was the deepest purple, she heard a sound that reminded her of scraping gravel. The geode split into two, nearly perfect halves as it rested in her hand. Clearly her mother had also conceded but wanted at least half of the amethyst.

Once her mom was buried, with the amethyst, Naomi would visit her own half of the stone frequently. One day while holding it, she received a clear image of her mother's twin sister. She knew her mom's twin needed healing, too. In the coming weeks, she found out that her mom's twin had fallen and fractured a vertebra and was in a great deal of pain. Naomi was confused and reluctant at first to let her half of the stone go. But she gave it to her mom's twin, who kept the amethyst by her bedside during her recovery, as a reminder of the twin sister who had physically passed on but continued to be by her side.

Protection

Some people fear that during certain activities, such as meditation and connecting to their intuition, they may be "opened up" to negative forces. The truth is that negative forces can be around us or in us at any time, and we may not be aware of it. Through your intuition you may simply become more aware of it. Your fear or negative expectations—*nocebo*—that something bad will happen, may weaken your mental and spiritual strength and quite literally your immune system and physical health.

By connecting to your intuition through the various exercises, you will become more aware of when you feel or experience positivity or negativity in any form—inside or outside of you. Then you will be more capable of addressing these positive and negative forces. You will be able to bring love, light, and positive energy to yourself and others around you with more focus and accuracy.

By connecting with positive feelings, prayers, and intention, you will be more protected from inner and outer negative forces. Fear and doubt can keep you from connecting to, listening to, and trusting your intuition. Therefore, if you feel it would help, go ahead and develop a protective routine prior to or in conjunction with connecting to your intuition. For example, you may want to say a prayer and set an intention to be safe and protected when listening to your intuition—and for all areas of your life, for that matter.

Intention is powerful. So if you are intending to connect with the most high and loving energies, then you will. Some will argue that these energies may fool you. I would argue that if you are in fear, you are already in a lower energy frequency and can be more easily fooled. That's why connecting with higher energies, such as love, will bring you better guidance and results of what you want to experience from your intuition.

You may find it helpful to pray to whatever spiritual or religious being or angel that may help you, asking them for protection. The Small Universe Meditation is a wonderful meditation to gather light around and in you and to cleanse and strengthen your energy, spirit, and aura. (See page 101.)

A Few More of My Stories

A fun and loving friend of mine was full of life and always had a large, comforting smile on her face. She was diagnosed with cancer and within two years died from it. After her death, she visited me in a dream. She was her same, happy self. Emphatically with kindness and a big smile, she said, "We don't die. I am fine. We don't die."

Seeing her and being with her in that dream felt more clear and real than "real" life. I felt at peace. I felt assured that there is more than this life. I now communicate with my friend and say hello whenever I think of her.

I learned that this is called a *visitation*, and this was one of my most profound, spiritually transformative experiences.

Another friend died of cancer. I recall listening to a song that we listened to together, and it made me think of him. One day, while I was running errands, I heard that song play. It made me think of him. I went to the next store. The same song was playing. How much could this be a coincidence? I went to the third location, and the same song was playing there. I started crying, as I knew that this was more than coincidence; this was beyond chance. This was his way of getting my attention and saying hello. I said hello to him in my mind and heart and felt connected to him. I felt him smiling at me and sending me love. I learned that when significant events or meaningful related experiences occur at the same time, it's called *synchronicity*.

In addition to connecting with loved ones after they have been here on earth, it seems possible that you may be visited by souls before they embody. I had this happen to me on three separate occasions with three new people who were about to come into the world. I dreamt of a family member's pregnancies before they knew they were pregnant and before any chance of an ultrasound, at only about four to six weeks pregnant. I had dreams of the children. I knew the sex, facial features, hair color, and personality of each child. To my astonishment, when I met each child at their own separate births at the hospital, I was saying hello, again, as I had already met them.

Universal Spirituality

You have spiritual gifts, learnings, and lessons no matter what path you choose. You may develop your spirituality within your own personal belief system or religious practice, or it may be separate, even if you consider yourself an atheist. All of these paths are similar, and no religion or spiritual practice is superior to another. We need to respect your and everyone's path and let go of the limiting belief that there is only one right way or that a particular way is better than another. This can actually create separation, more fear, and less love. In fact, many battles and wars have been fought over this in the name of "God."

Many believe one of the reasons we are here on this earth is to learn how to love. Some consider love interchangeable with God. All spiritual and religious practices teach love. Love is what unites us. Love is the glue that holds the universe together. Love is ultimately what we are all looking for—to be seen, valued, accepted, cared for, cherished or adored, treated with kindness, and to feel pleasure and connected instead of isolated and alone. We are looking to be unconditionally loved and accepted for who we are, to be unconditionally loving, and be believed and feel worthy in a way that can raise us and others to the highest heights. We are social creatures, and we need each other to survive, learn, and grow. If another person in our relationship sees our love and light, despite our seeming imperfections, this can connect us beyond our sense of separateness to something greater within and outside that can transcend limitations to boundless possibilities. This can give us strength, happiness, and peace.

Love and intuition can bring care, attention, and responsibility to care for and act on behalf of another, to come together and create a happier and healthier society. What you love to do, enjoy the most, and the creative gifts you bring to yourself and the world can help heal and keep us well, or allow us to cope well; these gifts may benefit the earth, environment, and all of its inhabitants.[25]

> *Love is the only force which can make things one without*
> *destroying them. . . . Some day, after mastering the winds,*
> *the waves, the tides, and gravity, we shall harness for God*
> *the energies of love, and then, for the second time in the*
> *history of the world, man will have discovered fire.*
> —PIERRE TEILHARD DE CHARDIN

Reflection:

What gives you meaning and purpose in life?

Do you feel connected to something greater than yourself?

What can help you to feel more meaning and purpose, more of a connection to something greater?

When do you feel the most loving?

When do you feel most loved?

Conclusion: Love and Intuition

You are like the sunshine. It can be blocked,
but it is never broken.
–Emmy Vadnais

Intuitive development is the journey to the heart. Love is the answer. The more you develop your intuition, the more loving you will be. As you live closer to your heart—with more love, wisdom, courage, and confidence, the easier it is for you to be intuitive. The more in tune you are with your intuition, the better you will feel. You will more confidently make good decisions. You will experience better health or a sense of wellness, joy, peace, contentment, and connection to your own greatness while feeling more alive. The more alive you feel, the more satisfying your relationships with yourself and others will be. The more satisfied you are, the more positive contributions you will offer to the world, in turn evoking a stronger personal sense of meaning and purpose.

By doing the exercises in this book, you will become more easily attuned to your natural intuitive senses, learning your strengths and cultivating ways to elicit the relaxation response. The more you listen to your intuitive gifts, the more they will grow and strengthen. The stronger they are, the more confident and comfortable you'll feel using your intuition.

If you are still questioning your abilities after having read this book, go back and do all of the exercises again. *You can't get full from only reading the menu*, some wise being said. Begin with the suggested exercises that seem small, less time consuming, or easy for you to do. Build from there. Then, practice an exercise at least three to five times per week, for a duration of twenty to thirty minutes, for at least six weeks. Research studies have shown that is the time required for the brain changes that occur from meditation—a practice correlated with intuitive abilities and positive states of being. As with beginning any new physical fitness routine, you need to give the practice time to strengthen the muscles before you will be fully aware of results. You need to exercise your *intuitive muscle* to experience the shift in your consciousness into intuitive awareness.

Make your intuitive cards. The subtleties you will discover in your intuitive deck will help you get in touch with the deepest parts of yourself. They will help you to fully experience all parts of yourself, including your intuition, helping you to discern what is intuition and what is not.

The more you open to receiving intuitive messages, the more likely and confident you will be to experience clear intuition. If you are doubting or questioning your intuition, or living in your head, or attached to too many emotions such as fear, you may block your intuition and it won't be as clear. It's best to be gentle with yourself as you cultivate your intuition. Say to yourself, "I trust my intuition and I'm doing the best I can as it becomes stronger for me." Realize you are learning; treat yourself with the understanding and patience you would give someone else who is learning something new. Judging or putting yourself down is unkind and destructive to growth. It's normal to have some doubt, because this is a new skill you are developing, but try to make a leap of faith and be open to the possibilities with your intuition. The opposite will only unwittingly block your progress. The better you know how you perceive your intuition, the more you can let go of distracting or conditioned emotions and tune in to true and accurate intuitive impressions, thoughts, feelings, emotions, and sensations.

Follow experiences in your life, present or past, in areas that are simple, and pay close attention to the developments as they unfold(ed), how you intuitively feel (felt) along the way, and the outcomes. Then you will have present or hindsight experiences that help you to understand when your intuition is or was speaking to you, versus worry, fear, doubt, or confusion. You will then be better able to discern the veracity of perceived information. Understand this is an ongoing process, and as you go forward you will fine-tune your intuitive perceptions to give you insight and help guide you forward in the best way possible.

Cultivate your witness consciousness—the part of you that's able to step back, that watches and observes, without any judgment or attachment, with unconditional love and acceptance. This takes practice. Even monks and wise spiritual leaders who have been practicing this for years are still cultivating this awareness, but it can grow each time you deliberately bring your attention to it. Regularly connect with your higher self and practice observing what is happening with neutral detachment, love, and compassion. When you do, you'll be able to see a situation more clearly and be open to the possibilities, versus being fixed on a preconceived outcome.

Connecting regularly with your intuition may actually help you heal, recover, or prevent disease. Regular relaxation and meditation practice can strengthen your energy, aliveness, and immune system. Your intuition may assist you to make healthy choices in your life, while simultaneously reducing stress that may have otherwise contributed to *dis-ease*. It can help you make wise, loving, and caring choices for yourself, those you care for, your loved ones, and everything that is meaningful in your life, giving you a more vibrant vitality.

Love and intuition go hand in hand: a loving state can expand your intuition, and being in your intuitive awareness can connect you to love. Having a truly open heart can allow the energy of love and intuition to flow more freely. You can then more easily access higher states of thinking and consciousness, such as intuition. You can act and make choices from your higher self that are intuitive and full of wisdom. When connected to our heart center, we can simply be present with ourselves and others with more loving, compassionate awareness. Spend time healing your heart, past wounds, hurts, or shame so you can more easily connect with your intuition and be a *clear channel*. Seek professional support to move past negative thoughts and beliefs, transforming them to positive ones.

If you would like support developing your intuition or are unsure of your gifts or abilities, seek out a teacher or practice partner. Studying and practicing with another person or group who would also like to develop their intuition is a great way to get practice, feedback, and support. This will help you trust your inner guidance and abilities. It can be a lot of fun to share this experience with another person or group. Being loved and witnessed by others as you discover parts of yourself can bring you a greater sense of love, connection, and acceptance. You may also help others, and doing so will bring more meaning, purpose, and joy to everyone involved.

My *Heart Group*, with our teacher, are four people who have been actively practicing with discipline in how to trust and gain confidence with our intuition. We have met regularly over the years and we have helped one another see past limitations to greater possibilities. My group has helped me gain confidence in my intuitive abilities by validating my intuitive impressions. The countless people I have helped develop their intuition have also tremendously helped me, but it was my teacher and my *Heart Group* that initially gave me the confidence to apply intuition to my personal life and to professionally help others. My heart has grown because of them, and I am forever grateful to them.

We all want to feel connected, loved, and united at our core. Your intuition and spirituality can help you to feel at home deeply within yourself, connected to and at one with something greater, as well as to all the inhabitants on earth. Your greater sense of peace, safety, faith, connectedness, sense of wonder, and love will help you to harmonize within yourself and with others. Your sense of greater love and connection may help put others at ease around you. You may have more fulfilling relationships and experiences in life. You will know what's working and have more tools to fix what's not, allowing evolution and learning. You'll help yourself, and you'll help heal society, culture, and the environment that provides the air we breathe, the water we drink, the food we eat, the beauty we enjoy, the nourishment of our souls, and so much more.

As you continue down your intuitive path, you will live more wholly and authentically. You will transform pain and anxiety to peace and joy, and align with the divine. You will feel more connected and at home with everything, everywhere. May you enjoy a deeper sense of joy, awe, wonder, and contentment that will grow for you every day.

Many blessings and much love to you,

Emmy

This above all: to thine own self be true,
And it must follow, as the night the day,
Thou canst not then be false to any man.
Farewell, my blessing season this in thee!
  –Shakespeare: *Hamlet*, Act I, Scene III

Endnotes by Chapter

Foreword Note

1. Cardeña, E. (2018). The experimental evidence for para-psychological phenomena: A review. *American Psychologist*, 73(5), 663–677. https://doi.org/10.1037/amp0000236

Introduction Note

1. Ornish, D. (2013, March 16). Opinion: Change your lifestyle, reverse your diseases. Retrieved April 17, 2018, from CNN website https://www.cnn.com/2013/03/16/opinion/ornish-health-lifystyle/

Chapter One Notes

1. Hodgkinson, G. P., Langan-Fox, J., & Sadler-Smith, E. (2008). Intuition: A fundamental bridging construct in the behavioural sciences. *British Journal of Psychology* (London, England: 1953), 99(Pt 1), 1–27. https://doi.org/10.1348/000712607X216666

2. Intuition. (n.d.). Definition retrieved May 10, 2018, from Lexico Dictionaries, English website https://www.lexico.com/en/definition/intuition

3. Intuition. (n.d.). Definition retrieved May 10, 2018, from https://www.merriam-webster.com/dictionary/intuition

4. Vadnais, E. (2018, September 1). *Science, magic, and intuition with Dean Radin, PhD* [video interview]. Retrieved from https://www.youtube.com/watch?v=iJ4KvP9JM4o&feature=youtu.be

5. McCraty, R. (2015). *Science of the heart, Vol. 2: Exploring the role of the heart in human performance* (1st ed.). HeartMath Institute.

6. Chapter 07: Intuition Research (n.d.). Retrieved May 10, 2018, from HeartMath Institute website https://www.heartmath.org/research/science-of-the-heart/intuition-research/

7. Myers, D. G. (2004). *Intuition: Its powers and perils*. New Haven, CT: Yale University Press.

8. Bradley, R., Gillin, L., McCraty, R., & Atkinson, M. (2011). Non-local intuition in entrepreneurs and non-entrepreneurs: Results of two experiments using electrophysiological measures. *International Journal of Entrepreneurship and Small Business, 12*. https://doi.org/10.1504/IJESB.2011.039012

9. Benson, H., & Stark, M. (1997). *Timeless healing: The power and biology of belief*. (reprint ed.). New York, NY: Fireside.

Chapter Two Notes

1. Killingsworth, M. A., & Gilbert, D. T. (2010). A wandering mind is an unhappy mind. *Science* (New York, NY), 330(6006), 932. https://doi.org/10.1126/science.1192439

2. Wallis, C. (2005, January 9). The new science of happiness. *Time*. Retrieved May 23, 2018, from http://content.time.com/time/magazine/article/0,9171,1015832-1,00.html

3. Benson, H., & Stark, M. (1997). *Timeless healing: The power and biology of belief*. (reprint ed.). New York, NY: Fireside.

4. Kim, H., & Sherman, D. (2007). "Express yourself": Culture and the effect of self-expression on choice. *Journal of Personality and Social Psychology, 92*, 1–11. https://doi.org/10.1037/0022-3514.92.1.1

5. Eubanks, D. L., Murphy, S. T., & Mumford, M. D. (2010). Intuition as an influence on creative problem-solving: the effects of intuition, positive affect, and training. *Creativity Research Journal, 22*(2), 170–184. https://doi.org/10.1080/10400419.2010.481513

6. Batey, P. (2011, February 7). Is creativity the number 1 skill for the 21st century? Retrieved May 23, 2018, from Psychology Today

website https://www.psychologytoday.com/us/blog/working
-creativity/201102/is-creativity-the-number-1-skill-the
-21st-century

7. Claxton, G. (1999). *Hare brain, tortoise mind: How intelligence
increases when you think less.* New York, NY: Harper
Perennial.

8. Hadamard, J. (1954). *The psychology of invention in the
mathematical field* (2nd ed.). New York, NY: Dover
Publications.

9. Gardner, H., & Nemirovsky, R. (1991). From private
intuitions to public symbol systems: An examination of
the creative process in Georg Cantor and Sigmund Freud.
Creativity Research Journal, 4(1), 1–21. https://doi.
org/10.1080/10400419109534370

10. Miller, A. I. (2000). *Insights of genius: Imagery and creativity in
science and art.* Cambridge, MA: MIT Press.

11. Isaacson, W. (2011, October 29). Opinion | The genius of jobs.
The New York Times. Retrieved from https://www.nytimes.
com/2011/10/30/opinion/sunday/steve-jobss-genius.html

12. Petervari, J., Osman, M., & Bhattacharya, J. (2016). The role of
intuition in the generation and evaluation stages of creativity.
Frontiers in Psychology, 7, 1420. https://doi.org/10.3389/
fpsyg.2016.01420

13. Csikszentmihalyi, M. (2008). *Flow: The psychology of optimal
experience* (1st ed.). (p. 74). New York, NY: Harper Perennial
Modern Classics.

14. Benson, H., & Proctor, W. (2011). *Relaxation revolution: The
science and genetics of mind body healing* (1st ed.). New York,
NY: Scribner.

15. Jordan, C. H., Whitfield, M., & Zeigler-Hill, V. (2007). Intuition
and the correspondence between implicit and explicit self-
esteem. *Journal of Personality and Social Psychology, 93*(6),
1067–1079. https://doi.org/10.1037/0022-3514.93.6.1067

16. Sansone, R. A., & Sansone, L. A. (2010). Gratitude and well being: The benefits of appreciation. *Psychiatry (Edgmont Township, PA), 7*(11), 18–22.

17. Rossman, M. L. (2011). *The worry solution: Using breakthrough brain science to turn stress and anxiety into confidence and happiness.* London: Rider Books.

18. Heal. (n.d.). Retrieved May 23, 2018, from https://www.merriam-webster.com/dictionary/heal

19. Vadnais, E. (2014, September 18). The power of the mind in healing. Retrieved May 23, 2018, from Holistic Occupational Therapy Community website https://holisticot.org/the-power-of-the-mind-in-healing-relaxation/

20. Bandelow, B., & Michaelis, S. (2015). Epidemiology of anxiety disorders in the 21st century. *Dialogues in Clinical Neuroscience, 17*(3), 327–335.

21. Remmers, C., & Zander, T. (2018). Why you don't see the forest for the trees when you are anxious: Anxiety impairs intuitive decision making. *Clinical Psychological Science, 6*(1), 48–62. https://doi.org/10.1177/2167702617728705

22. Lawrence, E. M., Rogers, R. G., & Wadsworth, T. (2015). Happiness and longevity in the United States. *Social Science & Medicine, 145*, 115–119. https://doi.org/10.1016/j.socscimed.2015.09.020

23. Ornish, D. (2013, March 16). Opinion: Change your lifestyle, reverse your diseases. Retrieved May 23, 2018, from CNN website https://www.cnn.com/2013/03/16/opinion/ornish-health-lifystyle/

24. Preventing chronic diseases: A vital investment. (n.d.). From the World Health Organization [Overview]. Retrieved November May 23, 2018, from WHO website http://www.who.int/chp/chronic_disease_report/part1/en/

25. Jeanne Achterberg quotes. [Author of *Woman as Healer*]. (n.d.).

Retrieved May 23, 2018, from https://www.goodreads.com
/author/quotes/101577.Jeanne_Achterberg

26. Burton, N. (2019, June 19). *These are the 7 types of love.*
Retrieved February 19, 2019, from Psychology Today website
https://www.psychologytoday.com/blog/hide-and-seek/201606
/these-are-the-7-types-love

27. Bridgen, E., & Verčič, D. (Eds.). (2018). *Experiencing public
relations: International voices.* New York, NY: Routledge,
Taylor & Francis Group.

28. Septimus, D. and Sabath Beit-Halachmi, R. (n.d.). Martin Buber.
Retrieved February 19, 2019, from My Jewish Learning website
https://www.myjewishlearning.com/article/martin-buber/

29. Greenberg, J. S. (2009). *Comprehensive stress management* (11th
ed.). New York, NY: McGraw-Hill.

Chapter Three Notes

1. Quantum physics—Latest research and news | Nature. (n.d.).
Retrieved June 11, 2018, from https://www.nature.com/
subjects/quantum-physics

2. Energy. (n.d.). Definition for English-Language Learners from
Merriam-Webster's Learner's Dictionary. Retrieved June 11,
2018, from http://www.learnersdictionary.com/definition/
energy

3. NOVA | Einstein's Big Idea | Library Resource Kit: E = mc2
Explained | PBS. (n.d.). Retrieved June 11, 2018 from https://
www.pbs.org/wgbh/nova/einstein/lrk-hand-emc2expl.html

4. Walia, A. (n.d.). Nothing is solid & everything is energy:
Scientists explain the world of quantum physics. Retrieved June
11, 2018, from Collective Evolution website https://www
.collective-evolution.com/2014/09/27/this-is-the-world-of-
quantum-physics-nothing-is-solid-and-everything-is-energy/

5. Physics: Newtonian physics (n.d.). from Encyclopedia.com.

Retrieved June 11, 2018, from https://www.encyclopedia.com
/science/science-magazines/physics-newtonian-physics

6. Vadnais, E. (2014, September 18). Energy flows where your
attention goes. Retrieved June 11, 2018, from Holistic
Occupational Therapy Community website https://holisticot
.org/energy-flows-attention-goes/

7. Reid, M. (2014, June 12). Einstein vs. quantum mechanics . . .
And why he'd be a convert today. Retrieved June 11, 2018
from The Conversation website http://theconversation.com/
einstein-vs-quantum-mechanics-and-why-hed-be-a-convert-
today-27641

8. Nonlocality and entanglement: Quantum theory and the
uncertainty principle—The physics of the universe. (n.d.).
Retrieved June 11, 2018, from The Physics of the Universe
website https://www.physicsoftheuniverse.com/topics_quantum
_nonlocality.html

9. Tate, K. (2013). How quantum entanglement works [Infographic].
Retrieved June 11, 2018, from Livescience.com website https://
www.livescience.com/28550-how-quantum-entanglement-
works-infographic.html

10. Fischer, D. B., Boes, A. D., Demertzi, A., Evrard, H. C., Laureys,
S., Edlow, B. L., . . . Geerling, J. C. (2016). A human brain
network derived from coma-causing brainstem lesions.
Neurology, 87(23), 2427–2434. https://doi.org/10.1212/WNL
.0000000000003404

11. The split brain experiments. [Educational games]. (2014).
Retrieved June 11, 2018 from Nobelprize.org website https://
educationalgames.nobelprize.org/educational/medicine/split-brain/

12. Cherry, K. (updated 2019, July 26). Left brain vs. right
brain: The surprising truth. Retrieved June 11, 2018, from
Verywell Mind website https://www.verywellmind.com/
left-brain-vs-right-brain-2795005

13. Nielsen, J. A., Zielinski, B. A., Ferguson, M. A., Lainhart, J. E.,

& Anderson, J. S. (2013). An evaluation of the left-brain vs. right-brain hypothesis with resting state functional connectivity magnetic resonance imaging. *PloS One, 8*(8), e71275. https://doi.org/10.1371/journal.pone.0071275

14. Doidge, N. (2007). *The Brain that changes itself: Stories of personal triumph from the frontiers of brain science* (Reprint ed.). London: Penguin Books.

15. Descartes, R. (1970). *The Philosophical writings of Descartes: Volume III*. New York, NY: Cambridge University Press.

16. Descartes, Rene. Internet Encyclopedia of Philosophy. (n.d.). Retrieved June 11, 2018, from https://www.iep.utm.edu/descarte/

17. Daher, J. C., Damiano, R. F., Lucchetti, A. L. G., Moreira-Almeida, A., & Lucchetti, G. (2017). Research on experiences related to the possibility of consciousness beyond the brain: A bibliometric analysis of global scientific output. *The Journal of Nervous and Mental Disease, 205*(1), 37–47. https://doi.org/10.1097/NMD.0000000000000625

18. Alexander, E., & Newell, K. (2017). *Living in a mindful universe: A neurosurgeon's journey into the heart of consciousness*. Emmaus, PA: Rodale Books.

19. Meijer, D., & Geesink, H. (2017). Consciousness in the universe is scale invariant and implies an event horizon of the human brain. *NeuroQuantology (September 2017) 153*, pp. 15, 41-79. https://doi.org/10.14704/nq.2017.15.3.1079

20. Thinking from the heart: Heart brain science. (n.d.). Retrieved June 11, 2018, from Noetic Systems International website http://noeticsi.com/thinking-from-the-heart-heart-brain-science/

21. Braden, G. (2015). *Resilience from the heart: The Power to thrive in life's extremes* (revised and updated ed.) (pp. 6-7). Carlsbad, CA: Hay House Inc.

22. The science of HeartMath. (2017, September 11). Retrieved June

11, 2018, from HeartMath Institute website https://www
.heartmath.com/science/

23. McCraty, R. (2003). The energetic heart: Bioelectromagnetic
communication within and between people. Retrieved June
11, 2018, from HeartMath Institute website https://www.
heartmath
.org/research/research-library/energetics/energetic-heart-bioelec
tromagnetic-communication-within-and-between-people/

24. The energetic heart is unfolding. (2010, July 22). Retrieved June
11, 2018, from HeartMath Institute website https://www.
heartmath.org/articles-of-the-heart/science-of-the-heart
/the-energetic-heart-is-unfolding/

25. Braden, G. (2015). *Resilience from the heart: The power to thrive
in life's extremes* (revised and updated ed.). Carlsbad, CA: Hay
House Inc.

26. McCraty, R. (2015). *Science of the heart: Exploring the role
of the human heart in human performance (Vol. 2)* (p. 5).
Boulder Creek, CA: HeartMath Institute.

27. Armour, J. A. (2003). *Neurocardiology: Anatomical and
functional principles* (pp. 1-2). Boulder Creek, CA: Institute of
HeartMath.

28. Braden, G. (2015). *Resilience from the heart: The power to
thrive in life's extremes* (revised and updated ed.) (pp. 11-13).
Carlsbad, CA: Hay House Inc.

29. Quick Coherence® Technique. Used with permission from
HeartMath Institute, https://www.heartmath.org

30. New Thinking Allowed with Jeffrey Mishlove. (2015, August 14).
[YouTube video]. Retrieved February 14, 2020, from YouTube
https://www.youtube.com/channel
/UCFk448YbGITLnzplK7jwNcw

Chapter Four Notes

1. The Piaget stages of cognitive development. (2018, May 25).

Retrieved June 28, 2018, from, The Psychology Notes
Headquarters website https://www.psychologynoteshq.com
/piagetstheory/

2. Arcane Bear. (2018, February 13). Supernormal and the
conscious universe—Dr. Dean Radin. [YouTube video].
Retrieved June 28, 2018, from https://www.youtube.com/
watch?v=6YjLWl4GBl0

3. Emotion. (n.d.). Definition retrieved June 28, 2018, from
Merriam-Webster website https://www.merriam-webster.com
/dictionary/emotion

4. Aron, E. N. (1997). *The highly sensitive person: How to thrive
when the world overwhelms you* (Reprint ed.). Portland, OR:
Broadway Books.

5. Radin, D. (2013). *Supernormal: Science, yoga, and the evidence
for extraordinary psychic abilities* (1st ed.) (pp. 89-90). New
York, NY: Deepak Chopra Books.

6. Achterberg, J. (1985). *Imagery in healing: Shamanism in modern
medicine* (Later print ed.) (pp. 4). Boston, MA: Shambhala.

7. Symbol. (n.d.). Definition retrieved June 28, 2018, from Merriam-
Webster website https://www.merriam-webster.com/dictionary
/symbol

8. Vadnais, E. (2011, October 6). *Special place imagery* [Video].
Retrieved June 28, 2018, from YouTube website https://youtu.
be/lgQbfEBagH8

Chapter Five Notes

1. Benson, H. & Klipper, M. (1975). T*he relaxation response*
(Reissue ed.) (pp. 4). New York, NY: HarperTorch.

2. Vadnais, E. (2014, September 18). The power of the mind in
healing. Retrieved July 19, 2018, from Holistic Occupational
Therapy Community website https://holisticot.org
/the-power-of-the-mind-in-healing-relaxation/

3. Jonas, W. (2018). *How healing works: Get well and stay well using your hidden power to heal* (1st ed.). California: Lorena Jones Books.

4. Alexander, E., & Newell, K. (2017). *Living in a mindful universe: A neurosurgeon's journey into the heart of consciousness.* Emmaus, PA: Rodale Books.

5. Schulte, B. (2015, May 26). Harvard neuroscientist: Meditation not only reduces stress, here's how it changes your brain. Retrieved July 19, 2018, from Washington Post website https://www.washingtonpost.com/news/inspired-life/wp/2015/05/26/harvard-neuroscientist-meditation-not-only-reduces-stress-it-literally-changes-your-brain/

6. Radin, D. (2018). *Real magic: Ancient wisdom, modern science, and a guide to the secret power of the universe* (1st ed.). New York, NY: Harmony Books.

7. Meditate. (n.d.). Definition retrieved July 19, 2018, from Merriam-Webster website https://www.merriam-webster.com/dictionary/meditate

8. Meditation, stress, and your health. (n.d.). Retrieved July 19, 2018, from WebMD website https://www.webmd.com/balance/guide/meditation-natural-remedy-for-insomnia#1

9. Nationwide survey reveals widespread use of mind and body practices. (2015, February 10). Retrieved July 19, 2018, from National Center for Complementary and Integrative Health website https://nccih.nih.gov/news/press/02102015mb

10. APA survey raises concern about health impact of stress on children and families. (2010, November 9). Retrieved July 19, 2018, from American Psychological Association website https://www.apa.org/news/press/releases/2010/11/stress-in-america

11. Stress in America: The state of our nation. (2017, November 1). [State-nation.pdf]. Retrieved July 19, 2018, from American Psychological Association website https://www.apa.org/news/press/releases/stress/2017/state-nation.pdf

12. Stress in America: Generation Z. Stress in America™ Survey. (2018, October). [Stress-gen-z.pdf]. Retrieved July 19, 2018, from American Psychological Association website https://www .apa.org/news/press/releases/stress/2018/stress-gen-z.pdf

13. Vadnais, E. (2015, April 6). 5 holistic pain relief approaches. Retrieved July 19, 2018, from Holistic Occupational Therapy Community website https://holisticot.org/5-holistic-pain -relief-approaches/

14. Radin, D. (2017, July). [Dean Radin—Bio]. Retrieved July 19, 2018, from DeanRadin.com website http://www.deanradin. com/NewWeb/bio.html

15. Radin, D. (2013). *Supernormal: Science, yoga, and the evidence for extraordinary psychic abilities* (1st ed., p. 323). New York, NY: Deepak Chopra Books.

16. Iyengar, B. K. S. (1979). *Light on yoga: Yoga dipika* (Revised ed.) (p. 19). New York, NY: Schocken Books.

17. Radin, D. (2013). *Supernormal: Science, yoga, and the evidence for extraordinary psychic abilities* (1st ed.) (p. 106). New York, NY: Deepak Chopra Books.

18. The Yoga sutras of Patanjali as-it-is: Introduction, commentaries, and translation. (n.d.). Retrieved February 4, 2019, from RainbowBody.Net website http://www.rainbowbody.net/Heart Mind/Yogasutra.htm

19. Yoga for high blood pressure. (n.d.). Retrieved February 4, 2019, from Yoga Journal website https://www.yogajournal.com/poses /yoga-by-benefit/high-blood-pressure

20. Schmid, A., & van Puymbroeck, M. (2019). *Yoga therapy for stroke: A handbook for yoga therapists and healthcare professionals* (1st ed.). London and Philadelphia: Singing Dragon.

21. Stachowiak, Julie. (Updated 2019, November 16). Complementary and alternative medicine for multiple sclerosis. Retrieved February 4, 2019, from Verywell Health website https://www.verywellhealth.com/cam-for-ms-24404e

22. Poland, K. P. (2015, July 1). Yoga for Parkinson's: What the research says. Retrieved February 4, 2019, from The Michael J. Fox Foundation for Parkinson's Research website https://www.michaeljfox.org/news/yoga-parkinsons-what-research-says?yoga-for-parkinson-what-the-research-says=

23. Woodyard, C. (2011). Exploring the therapeutic effects of yoga and its ability to increase quality of life. *International Journal of Yoga*, 4(2), 49–54. https://doi.org/10.4103/0973-6131.85485

24. Scott, E. (Updated 2019, August 28). 17 highly effective stress relievers. Retrieved February 4, 2019, from Verywell Mind website https://www.verywellmind.com/tips-to-reduce-stress-3145195

Chapter Six Notes

1. Benson, H., & Proctor, W. (2011). *Relaxation revolution: The science and genetics of mind body healing* (1st ed., pp. 9-10). New York, NY: Scribner.

2. Neff, K. D. (2011). Self-compassion, self-esteem, and well-being. *Social and personality psychology compass,* 5(1), 1–12. https://doi.org/10.1111/j.1751-9004.2010.00330.x

3. Compassion. (n.d.). Definition retrieved September 7, 2018, from Merriam-Webster website https://www.merriam-webster.com/dictionary/compassion

4. What is compassion. (n.d.). Definition retrieved September 7, 2018, from Greater Good website https://greatergood.berkeley.edu/topic/compassion/definition

5. Marsh, J. (2013, May 23). How to train the compassionate brain. Retrieved September 7, 2018, from Greater Good website https://greatergood.berkeley.edu/article/item/how_to_train_the_compassionate_brain

6. Forgas, J. P., & Bower, G. H. (1987). Mood effects on person-perception judgments. *Journal of Personality and Social*

Psychology, 53(1), 53–60. https://doi.org
/10.1037//0022-3514.53.1.53

7. Neff, K. (2015, September 30). The five myths of self-compassion. Retrieved September 7, 2018, from Greater Good website https://greatergood.berkeley.edu/article/item/the_five_myths_of_self_compassion

8. Winner, J. (2008, October 29). Decenter to be centered. Retrieved September 7, 2018, from Psychology Today website http://www.psychologytoday.com/blog/stress-remedy/200810/decenter-be-centered

9. Stahl, B., Goldstein, E., & Santorelli, S. (2010). *A Mindfulness-based stress reduction workbook* (Workbook ed.) (p. 15). Oakland, CA: New Harbinger Publications.

10. Kuyken, W., Warren, F. C., Taylor, R. S., Whalley, B., Crane, C., Bondolfi, G., . . . Dalgleish, T. (2016). Efficacy of mindfulness-based cognitive therapy in prevention of depressive relapse: An individual patient data meta-analysis from randomized trials. *JAMA Psychiatry, 73*(6), 565–574. https://doi.org/10.1001/jamapsychiatry.2016.0076

11. Hoge, E. A., Bui, E., Marques, L., Metcalf, C. A., Morris, L. K., Robinaugh, D. J., . . . Simon, N. M. (2013). Randomized controlled trial of mindfulness meditation for generalized anxiety disorder: Effects on anxiety and stress reactivity. *The Journal of Clinical Psychiatry, 74*(8), 786–792. https://doi.org/10.4088/JCP.12m08083

12. Wake Forest Baptist Medical Center. Mindfulness meditation provides opioid-free pain relief, study finds. (2016, March 15). Retrieved September 7, 2018, from ScienceDaily website https://www.sciencedaily.com/releases/2016/03/160315182706.htm

13. Burnout. (n.d.). Definition retrieved September 7, 2018, from Merriam-Webster website https://www.merriam-webster.com

/dictionary/burnout

14. Luken, M., & Sammons, A. (2016). Systematic review of mindfulness practice for reducing job burnout. *The American Journal of Occupational Therapy, 70*(2), 7002250020p1-7002250020p10. https://doi.org/10.5014/ajot.2016.016956

15. Jon Kabat-Zinn: About the author. (n.d.). Retrieved September 7, 2018, from https://www.mindfulnesscds.com/pages/about-the-author

16. Hofmann, S. G., Grossman, P., & Hinton, D. E. (2011). Loving-kindness and compassion meditation: Potential for psychological interventions. *Clinical Psychology Review, 31*(7), 1126–1132. https://doi.org/10.1016/j.cpr.2011.07.003

17. Condon, P., Desbordes, G., Miller, W. B., & DeSteno, D. (2013). Meditation increases compassionate responses to suffering. *Psychological Science, 24*(10), 2125–2127. https://doi.org/10.1177/0956797613485603

18. Land, D. (2008, March 25). Study shows compassion meditation changes the brain. Retrieved September 7, 2018, from University of Wisconsin-Madison News website https://news.wisc.edu/study-shows-compassion-meditation-changes-the-brain/

19. Pannyavaro, V. (n.d.). Overview of loving-kindness meditation. Retrieved September 7, 2018, from http://www.buddhanet.net/metta_in.htm

20. Kornfield, J. (2008). *The art of forgiveness, lovingkindness, and peace* (Paperback ed.) (pp. 117-121). New York, NY: Bantam Dell.

21. Jung, C. G., & Chodorow, J. (1997). *Jung on active imagination* (p. 145). Princeton, NJ: Princeton University Press.

22. Cleveland Clinic. Guided imagery.(n.d.). Retrieved September 7, 2018, from Cleveland Clinic website https://my.clevelandclinic.org/departments/wellness/integrative/treatments-services/

guided-imagery

23. Achterberg, J. (1985). *Imagery in healing: Shamanism in modern medicine* (Later print ed.). Boston, MA: Shambhala.

Chapter Seven Notes

1. Sundermier, A. (2016, September 23). 99.9999999% of your body is empty space. Retrieved February 6, 2019, from ScienceAlert website https://www.sciencealert.com/99-9999999-of-your -body-is-empty-space

2. Judith, A. (2016). *Wheels of life: A user's guide to the chakra system* (2nd ed.). St. Paul, MN: Llewellyn Publications.

3. Feuerstein, G. (2000). *Shambhala encyclopedia of yoga*. Boston, MA: Shambhala.

4. Tigunait, P. R. (1998). *Sakti: The power in tantra: A scholarly approach*. Honesdale, PA: Himalayan Institute Press.

5. Feynman, R. P., Leighton, R. B., & Sands, M. L. (1963). *The Feynman lectures on physics*. Reading, MA: Addison-Wesley Pub. Co.

6. Chevalier, G., Sinatra, S., Oschman, J., Sokal, K., & Sokal, P. (2012). Earthing: Health implications of reconnecting the human body to the earth's surface electrons. *Journal of Environmental and Public Health*, 2012, 291541. https://doi .org/10.1155/2012/291541

7. DiNucci, E. M. (2005). Energy healing: A complementary treatment for orthopaedic and other conditions. *Orthopedic Nursing, 24*(4), 259–269. https://doi.org/10.1097/00006416 -200507000-00006

8. Birocco, N., Guillame, C., Storto, S., Ritorto, G., Catino, C., Gir, N., . . . Ciuffreda, L. (2012). The effects of reiki therapy on pain and anxiety in patients attending a day oncology and infusion services unit. *The American Journal of Hospice & Palliative Care, 29*(4), 290–294. https://doi. org/10.1177/1049909111420859

9. Acupuncture: In depth. (2008, January 1). Retrieved August 19, 2019, from National Center for Complementary and Integrative Health website https://nccih.nih.gov/health/acupuncture/introduction

10. Mist, S. D., Aickin, M., Kalnins, P., Cleaver, J., Batchelor, R., Thorne, T., . . . Colbert, A. P. (2011). Reliability of AcuGraph system for measuring skin conductance at acupoints. *Acupuncture in Medicine, 29*(3), 221–226. https://doi.org/10.1136/aim.2010.003012

Chapter Eight Notes

1. Achterberg, J. (1985). *Imagery in healing: Shamanism in modern medicine* (Later print ed.). Boston, MA: Shambhala.

2. Jung, C. G., & Chodorow, J. (1997). *Jung on active imagination.* Princeton, NJ: Princeton University Press.

3. Jung, C. G., von Franz, M., Henderson, J. L., Jacobi, J., & Jaffé, A. (1964). *Man and his symbols.* New York, NY: Dell Publishing.

4. Jung, C. G. (1990). *The archetypes and the collective unconscious* (2nd ed.; R. F. C. Hull, trans.). New York, NY: Princeton University Press.

5. von Petzinger, G. (2017). *The first signs: Unlocking the mysteries of the world's oldest symbols* (Reprint ed.). New York, NY: Atria Books.

6. Fontana, D. (1994). *The secret language of symbols: A visual key to symbols and their meanings.* San Francisco, CA: Chronicle Books.

7. Scoville, P. (2015, July 2). Egyptian hieroglyphs. Definition retrieved May 17, 2019, from Ancient History Encyclopedia website https://www.ancient.eu/Egyptian_Hieroglyphs/

8. Campbell, J., & Moyers, B. (1988). *The power of myth* (pp. 4-5). New York, NY: Anchor Books.

9. Campbell, J. (2008). *The hero with a thousand faces* (3rd ed.). Novato, CA: New World Library.

10. Ratcliffe, A. (2016, July 25). 6 great quotes about the force. Retrieved May 17, 2019, from StarWars.com website https://www.starwars.com/news/6-great-quotes-about-the-force

11. Brennan, Kristen. Star Wars origins—Joseph Campbell and the hero's journey. (n.d.). Retrieved May 17, 2019, from http://www.moongadget.com/origins/myth.html

12. Plot of Star Wars: Episode IV - A New Hope (1977). (n.d.). Retrieved May 17, 2019, from IMDb website http://www.imdb.com/title/tt0076759/plotsummary

13. Eakins, P. (1992). *Tarot of the spirit*. York Beach, ME: Samuel Weiser, Inc.

14. Arrien, A. (1987). *The tarot handbook: Practical applications of ancient visual symbols*. (p. 18). New York, NY: Jeremy P. Tarcher/Putnam.

15. Wing, R. L. (1979). *The I Ching workbook*. [Back cover]. Garden City, NY: Doubleday & Company, Inc.

16. Parker, J., & Parker, D. (2001). *Parker's astrology: The definitive guide to using astrology in every aspect of your life*. (2nd ed.). New York, NY: DK Publishing, Inc.

Chapter Nine Notes

1. Eakins, P. (1992). *Tarot of the spirit* (p. 24). York Beach, ME: Samuel Weiser, Inc.

2. Malchiodi, C. A. (2007). *The art therapy sourcebook*. (2nd ed.). New York, NY: McGraw-Hill.

3. Jung, C. G., von Franz, M. Henderson, J. L., Jacobi, J., & Jaffé, A. (1964). *Man and his symbols*. New York, NY: Dell Publishing.

Chapter Ten Notes

1. Radin, D. (2018). *Real magic: Ancient wisdom, modern science, and a guide to the secret power of the universe*. (1st ed.) (p. 145). New York, NY: Harmony Books.

2. Grabhorn, L. (2000). *Excuse me, your life is waiting: The astonishing power of feelings.* Charlottesville, VA: Hampton Roads Pub. Co.

3. Hill, N., & Pell, A. R. (2005). *Think and grow rich.* New York, NY: Jeremy P. Tarcher/Penguin.

4. Jarrett, R. H. (1992). *It works: The famous little red book that makes your dreams come true!* (31st ed.). New York, NY: Devorss & Co.

5. Unknown. (n.d.). I sent you a rowboat. Retrieved May 13, 2019, from Stories for Preaching website https://storiesforpreaching.com/i-sent-you-a-rowboat/

6. Frank, C., Land, W. M., Popp, C., & Schack, T. (2014). Mental representation and mental practice: Experimental investigation on the functional links between motor memory and motor imagery. *PloS One, 9*(4), e95175. https://doi.org/10.1371/journal.pone.0095175

7. Benson, H., & Proctor, W. (2011). *Relaxation revolution: The science and genetics of mind body healing* (1st ed.). New York, NY: Scribner.

8. Krause, N., & Hayward, R. D. (2013). Prayer beliefs and change in life satisfaction over time. *Journal of Religion and Health, 52*(2), 674–694. https://doi.org/10.1007/s10943-012-9638-1

9. Benson, H., & Stark, M. (1997). *Timeless healing: The power and biology of belief.* (Reprint ed.). New York, NY: Fireside.

10. Sansone, R. A., & Sansone, L. A. (2010). Gratitude and well being: The benefits of appreciation. *Psychiatry (Township PA), 7*(11), 18–22.

11. Chesmark, C. A. (2018). *How to predict the future by creating it yourself: The user's manual for your subconscious mind.* Publisher: Chad Chesmark

12. Youssef, N. A., Lockwood, L., Su, S., Hao, G., & Rutten, B. P. F. (2018). The effects of trauma, with or without PTSD, on the transgenerational DNA methylation alterations in human

offsprings. *Brain Sciences, 8*(5). https://doi.org/10.3390/
brainsci8050083

13. Caiola, R. (2016, March 10). How experiences change
    markers in our DNA. Retrieved May 20, 2019, from
    Rewire Me website https://www.rewireme.com/insight/
    experiences-change-markers/

14. Jonas, W. (2018). *How healing works: Get well and stay well
    using your hidden power to heal* (1st ed.). California: Lorena
    Jones Books.

15. Strecher, V. J. (2016). *Life on purpose: How living for what
    matters most changes everything* (1st ed.). New York, NY:
    HarperOne.

16. Energy psychology—Association for Comprehensive Energy
    Psychology. (n.d.). Retrieved November 17, 2019, from
    Association for Comprehensive Energy Psychology website
    https://www.energypsych.org/page/AboutEPv2

17. Hartmann, S. (2002). Practitioner of meridian energy therapies
    certification training manual. The Association for Meridian
    Energy Therapies website https://goe.ac/ (previously, theamt.
    com)

18. Herbst, B. (2019, January 29). Purpose versus mission in
    astrology: Part one. Retrieved May 15, 2019, from Bill Herbst
    website https://billherbst.com/Comm131.pdf

19. Herbst, B. (2019, February 5). Purpose versus mission in
    astrology: Part two. Retrieved May 15, 2019, from Bill Herbst
    website https://billherbst.com/Comm132.pdf

20. Herbst, B. (2019, February 12). Purpose versus mission in
    astrology: Part three. Retrieved May 15, 2019, from Bill Herbst
    website https://billherbst.com/Comm133.pdf

21. Anonymous. (n.d.). Ecclesiastes 3:1-8. Retrieved May 15, 2019,
    from The Academy of American Poets website https://poets.org
    /poem/ecclesiastes-31-8

Chapter Eleven Notes

1. Spirit. (2019). In Wikipedia. Retrieved July 26, 2019, from, https://en.wikipedia.org/w/index.php?title=Spirit&oldid=925896711

2. When Americans say they believe in God, what do they mean? (2018, April 25). Retrieved May 10, 2019, from Pew Research Center's Religion & Public Life Project website https://www.pewforum.org/2018/04/25/when-americans-say-they-believe-in-god-what-do-they-mean/

3. Poll: Nearly 8 in 10 Americans believe in angels. (2011, December 23). Retrieved May 10, 2019, from CBS News website https://www.cbsnews.com/news/poll-nearly-8-in-10-americans-believe-in-angels/

4. Morgan, M. (2016, April 25). 90% of Americans have prayed for healing, study finds. Retrieved May 10, 2019, from CNN website https://www.cnn.com/2016/04/25/health/healing-power-of-prayer-study/index.html

5. American Occupational Therapy Association. Occupational therapy practice framework: Domain & process. (2008). (2nd ed.) *American Journal of Occupational Therapy, 62*(6), 625–683. https://doi.org/10.5014/ajot.62.6.625

6. Clinebell, H. J. (1992). *Well being: A personal plan for exploring and enriching the seven dimensions of life: Mind, body, spirit, love, work, play, the earth.* New York, NY: Harper Collins.

7. Seven spiritual needs. (n.d.). Retrieved July 15, 2019, from University of Minnesota website https://www.takingcharge.csh.umn.edu/enhance-your-wellbeing/purpose/spirituality/seven-spiritual-needs

8. *Holy Bible: New international version.* (2011). Grand Rapids, MI: Zondervan Publishing House.

9. Prophet. (n.d.). Definition retrieved June 4, 2019, from Merriam-Webster website https://www.merriam-webster.com/thesaurus/prophet

10. Bodine, E. (n.d.). The gift of prophecy. Retrieved June 4, 2019, from The Intuitive-Connections Network website http://www .intuitive-connections.net/2006/book-key.htm

11. Mystic. (n.d.). Definition retrieved June 24, 2019, from Dictionary.com website https://www.dictionary.com/browse/ mystic

12. Armstrong, K. (1993). *A history of God: The 4000-year quest of Judaism, Christianity and Islam*. New York, NY: Ballantine Books.

13. Oracle. (n.d.). Definition retrieved July 24, 2019, from Merriam-Webster website https://www.merriam-webster.com/dictionary/ oracle

14. Cartwright, M. (2013, February 22). Delphi. Retrieved July 24, 2019, from Ancient History Encyclopedia website https://www .ancient.eu/delphi/

15. Archaeological site of Delphi. (n.d.). Retrieved July 24, 2019, from World Heritage Convention-UNESCO website https:// whc.unesco.org/en/list/393/

16. Emmy Vadnais. (2019, June 4). [Facebook post]. Retrieved from Facebook July 24 2019 from https://www.facebook.com/ emmyvadnais

17. Shannon, J. (n.d.). [Personal exchange]. Changing how we feel by changing how we think. Institute for Brain Potential.

18. Learning Modules for Healthcare Professionals. (2015, October 20). Retrieved July 24, 2019, from University of Minnesota Center for Spirituality and Healing website. https://www.csh. umn.edu/education/online-modules-and-resources/learning -modules-healthcare-professionals

19. Benson, H., & Stark, M. (1997). *Timeless healing: The power and biology of belief*. (Reprint ed.). New York, NY: Fireside.

20. Ātman (Hinduism). (2019). Retrieved June 4, 2019, from Wikipedia https://en.wikipedia.org/w/index.php?title=%C4 %80tman_(Hinduism)&oldid=925519445

21. Brahman. (2019). Retrieved June 4, 2019, from Wikipedia https://en.wikipedia.org/w/index.php?title=Brahman&oldid=926224960

22. Vedas. (2019). Retrieved June 4, 2019, from Wikipedia https://en.wikipedia.org/w/index.php?title=Vedas&oldid=926461124

23. Moody, R. A. (2015). *Life after life: The bestselling original investigation that revealed "near-death experiences."* (Anniversary, special ed.). New York, NY: HarperOne.

24. Dr. Raymond Moody Talks About Near-Death Experiences. (2016, September 16). Guideposts [YouTube video]. Retrieved February 19, 2019, from https://www.youtube.com/watch?v=WYuniH2jYRI

25. Jonas, W. (2018). *How healing works: Get well and stay well using your hidden power to heal.* (1st ed.). California: Lorena Jones Books.

Bibliography

Achterberg, J. (2002). *Imagery in healing: Shamanism and modern medicine* (1st ed.). Boulder, Colorado: Shambhala.

Alexander, E. (2012). *Proof of heaven: A neurosurgeon's journey into the afterlife* (1st hardcover ed.). New York, NY: Simon & Schuster.

Alexander, E., & Newell, K. (2017). *Living in a mindful universe: A neurosurgeon's journey into the heart of consciousness.* Emmaus, PA: Rodale Books.

Austill-Clausen, R. (2016) *Change maker: how my brother's death woke up my life.* Berkeley, CA: She Writes Press.

American Occupational Therapy Association. Occupational therapy practice framework: Domain & process. (2008). (2nd ed.) *American Journal of Occupational Therapy*, 62(6), 625–683. https://doi.org/10.5014/ajot.62.6.625

Armstrong, K. (1993). *A history of God: The 4000-year quest of Judaism, Christianity and Islam.* New York, NY: Ballantine Books.

Aron, E. N. (2017). *The highly sensitive person: How to thrive when the world overwhelms you.* (Reprint ed.). Portland, OR: Broadway Books.

Arrien, A. (1987). *The tarot handbook: Practical applications of ancient visual symbols.* New York, NY: Jeremy P. Tarcher/ Putnam.

Bandelow, B., & Michaelis, S. (2015). Epidemiology of anxiety disorders in the 21st century. *Dialogues in Clinical Neuroscience*, 17(3), 327–335.

Benson, H., & Klipper, M. (1975). *The relaxation response* (Reissue ed.). New York, NY: HarperTorch.

Benson, H., & Proctor, W. (2011). *Relaxation revolution: The science and genetics of mind body healing* (1st ed.). New York, NY: Scribner.

Benson, H., & Stark, M. (1997). *Timeless healing: The power and biology of belief.* (Reprint ed.). New York, NY: Fireside.

Birocco, N., Guillame, C., Storto, S., Ritorto, G., Catino, C., Gir, N., . . . Ciuffreda, L. (2012). The effects of reiki therapy on pain and anxiety in patients attending a day oncology and infusion services unit. *The American Journal of Hospice & Palliative Care*, 29(4), 290–294. https://doi.org/10.1177/1049909111420859

Braden, G. (2015). *Resilience from the heart: The power to thrive in life's extremes* (revised and updated ed.). Carlsbad, CA: Hay House Inc.

Bradley, R., Gillin, L., McCraty, R., & Atkinson, M. (2011). Non-local intuition in entrepreneurs and non-entrepreneurs: Results of two experiments using electrophysiological measures. *International Journal of Entrepreneurship and Small Business*, 12. https://doi.org/10.1504/IJESB.2011.039012

Bridgen, E., & Verčič, D. (eds.). (2018). *Experiencing public relations: International voices.* New York, NY: Routledge, Taylor & Francis Group.

Campbell, J. (2008). *The hero with a thousand faces* (3rd ed.). Novato, CA: New World Library.

Campbell, J., & Moyers, B. D. (1988). *The power of myth.* New York, NY: Doubleday.

Cardeña, E. (2018). The experimental evidence for parapsychological phenomena: A review. *American Psychologist*, 73(5), 663–677. https://doi.org/10.1037/amp0000236

Chesmark, C. A. (2018). *How to predict the future by creating it yourself: The user's manual for your subconscious mind.* Publisher: Chad Chesmark.

Chevalier, G., Sinatra, S., Oschman, J., Sokal, K., & Sokal, P. (2012). Earthing: Health implications of reconnecting the human body to the earth's surface electrons. *Journal of Environmental and Public Health*, 2012, 291541. https://doi.org/10.1155/2012/291541

Claxton, G. (1999). *Hare brain, tortoise mind: How intelligence increases when you think less*. New York, NY: Harper Perennial.

Clinebell, H. J. (1992). *Well being: A personal plan for exploring and enriching the seven dimensions of life: mind, body, spirit, love, work, play, the earth*. New York, NY: Harper Collins.

Csikszentmihalyi, M. (2009). *Flow: The psychology of optimal experience* (1st ed.). New York, NY: Harper Perennial Modern Classics.

Condon, P., Desbordes, G., Miller, W. B., & DeSteno, D. (2013). Meditation increases compassionate responses to suffering. *Psychological Science*, 24(10), 2125–2127. https://doi.org/10.1177/0956797613485603

Daher, J. C., Damiano, R. F., Lucchetti, A. L. G., Moreira-Almeida, A., & Lucchetti, G. (2017). Research on experiences related to the possibility of consciousness beyond the brain: A bibliometric analysis of global scientific output. *The Journal of Nervous and Mental Disease*, 205(1), 37–47. https://doi.org/10.1097/NMD.0000000000000625

Dass, R. (1978). *Be here now: Remember*. New York, NY: Crown Publishing Group.

Descartes, R. (1970). *The philosophical writings of Descartes: Volume III*. New York, NY: Cambridge University Press.

DiNucci, E. M. (2005). Energy healing: A complementary treatment for orthopaedic and other conditions. *Orthopedic Nursing*, 24(4), 259–269. https://doi.org/10.1097/00006416-200507000-00006

Dispenza, D. J. (2017) *Becoming Supernatural: How Common People are Doing the Uncommon*. Hay House Inc.

Dispenza, D. J. (2012). *Breaking the Habit of Being Yourself: How to Lose Your Mind and Create a New One*; also *Becoming Supernatural*. UK: Hay House Inc.

Dispenza, D. J. (2015). *You are the placebo: Making your mind matter* (reprint ed.). Carlsbad, CA: Hay House Inc.

Doidge, N. (2008). *The brain that changes itself: Stories of personal triumph from the frontiers of brain science* (reprint ed.). London: Penguin Books.

Dossey, L. (2013). *One mind: How our individual mind is part of a greater consciousness and why it matters*. Carlsbad, CA: Hay House, Inc.

Eakins, P. (1992). *Tarot of the spirit*. York Beach, ME: Samuel Weiser, Inc.

Eisner, D. (2016) *The clinical success formula: how to reduce anxiety, build confidence, and pass with flying colors*. Dan Eisner Consulting.

Eubanks, D. L., Murphy, S. T., & Mumford, M. D. (2010). Intuition as an influence on creative problem-solving: the effects of intuition, positive affect, and training. *Creativity Research Journal*, 22(2), 170–184. https://doi.org/10.1080/10400419.2 010.481513

Feuerstein, G. (2000). *The Shambhala encyclopedia of yoga*. Boston, MA: Shambhala.

Feynman, R. P., Leighton, R. B., Sands, M., Gottlieb, M. A., & Leighton, R. (eds.). (2006). *The Feynman lectures on physics* (definitive ed.). San Francisco, CA: Pearson, Addison-Wesley.

Fischer, D. B., Boes, A. D., Demertzi, A., Evrard, H. C., Laureys, S., Edlow, B. L., . . . Geerling, J. C. (2016). A human brain network derived from coma-causing brainstem lesions. *Neurology*, 87(23), 2427–2434. https://doi.org/10.1212/ WNL.0000000000003404

Forgas, J. P., & Bower, G. H. (1987). Mood effects on person-perception judgments. *Journal of Personality and Social Psychology*, 53(1), 53–60. https://doi.org/10.1037//0022-3514.53.1.53

Fontana, D. (1994). *The secret language of symbols: A visual key to symbols and their meanings.* San Francisco, CA: Chronicle Books.

Frank, C., Land, W. M., Popp, C., & Schack, T. (2014). Mental representation and mental practice: Experimental investigation on the functional links between motor memory and motor imagery. *PloS One*, 9(4), e95175. https://doi.org/10.1371/journal.pone.0095175

Gach, M. R., & Henning, B. A. (2004). *Acupressure for emotional healing: A self-care guide for trauma, stress & common emotional imbalances.* New York, NY: Bantam Books.

Gardner, H., & Nemirovsky, R. (1991). From private intuitions to public symbol systems: An examination of the creative process in Georg Cantor and Sigmund Freud. *Creativity Research Journal*, 4(1), 1–21. https://doi.org/10.1080/10400419109534370

Grabhorn, L. (2000). *Excuse me, your life is waiting: The astonishing power of feelings.* Charlottesville, VA: Hampton Roads Pub. Co.

Greenberg, J. S. (2009). *Comprehensive stress management* (11th ed.). New York, NY: McGraw-Hill.

Hadamard, J. (1954). *An essay on the psychology of invention in the mathematical field* (Dover ed.). Princeton, NJ: Princeton University Press.

Hill, N., & Pell, A. R. (2005). *Think and grow rich* (1st ed.). New York, NY: Jeremy P. Tarcher/Penguin.

Hodgkinson, G. P., Langan-Fox, J., & Sadler-Smith, E. (2008). Intuition: A fundamental bridging construct in the behavioural sciences. *British Journal of Psychology*

(London, England: 1953), 99(Pt 1), 1–27. https://doi.
org/10.1348/000712607X216666

Hoge, E. A., Bui, E., Marques, L., Metcalf, C. A., Morris, L. K.,
Robinaugh, D. J., . . . Simon, N. M. (2013). Randomized
controlled trial of mindfulness meditation for generalized
anxiety disorder: Effects on anxiety and stress reactivity. *The
Journal of Clinical Psychiatry*, 74(8), 786–792. https://doi.
org/10.4088/JCP.12m08083

Hofmann, S. G., Grossman, P., & Hinton, D. E. (2011).
Loving-kindness and compassion meditation: Potential for
psychological interventions. *Clinical Psychology Review*, 31(7),
1126–1132. https://doi.org/10.1016/j.cpr.2011.07.003

Holy Bible: New international version (textbook ed.). (2011). Grand
Rapids, MI: Zondervan Publishing House.

Isaacson, W. (2011, October 29). Opinion | The genius of jobs.
The New York Times. Retrieved from https://www.nytimes.
com/2011/10/30/opinion/sunday/steve-jobss-genius.html

Iyengar, B. K. S. (1979). *Light on yoga: Yoga dipika* (revised ed.).
New York, NY: Schocken Books.

Jarrett, R. H. (2016). *It works: The famous little red book that makes
your dreams come true!* (31st ed.). New York, NY: Devorss & Co.

Jonas, W. (2018). *How healing works: Get well and stay well using
your hidden power to heal* (1st ed.). California: Lorena Jones
Books.

Jordan, C. H., Whitfield, M., & Zeigler-Hill, V. (2007). Intuition
and the correspondence between implicit and explicit self-
esteem. *Journal of Personality and Social Psychology*, 93(6),
1067–1079. https://doi.org/10.1037/0022-3514.93.6.1067

Judith, A. (2016). *Wheels of life: A user's guide to the chakra system*
(2nd ed.). St. Paul, MN: Llewellyn Publications.

Jung, C. G., & Chodorow, J. (1997). *Jung on active imagination*.
Princeton, NJ: Princeton University Press.

Jung, C. G., von Franz, M., Henderson, J. L., Jacobi, J., & Jaffé, A. (1964). *Man and his symbols*. New York, NY: Dell Publishing.

Jung, C. G. (1990). *The archetypes and the collective unconscious* (2nd ed.; R. F. C. Hull, trans). New York, NY: Princeton University Press.

Killingsworth, M. A., & Gilbert, D. T. (2010). A wandering mind is an unhappy mind. *Science* (New York, NY), 330(6006), 932. https://doi.org/10.1126/science.1192439

Kim, H., & Sherman, D. (2007). "Express yourself": Culture and the effect of self-expression on choice. *Journal of Personality and Social Psychology*, 92, 1–11. https://doi.org/10.1037/0022-3514.92.1.1

Kornfield, J. (2002). *The art of forgiveness, lovingkindess, and peace* (paperback ed.). New York, NY: Bantam Dell.

Krause, N., & Hayward, R. D. (2013). Prayer beliefs and change in life satisfaction over time. *Journal of Religion and Health*, 52(2), 674–694. https://doi.org/10.1007/s10943-012-9638-1

Kuyken, W., Warren, F. C., Taylor, R. S., Whalley, B., Crane, C., Bondolfi, G., . . . Dalgleish, T. (2016). Efficacy of mindfulness-based cognitive therapy in prevention of depressive relapse: An individual patient data meta-analysis from randomized trials. *JAMA Psychiatry*, 73(6), 565–574. https://doi.org/10.1001/jamapsychiatry.2016.0076

Lawrence, E. M., Rogers, R. G., & Wadsworth, T. (2015). Happiness and longevity in the United States. *Social Science & Medicine, 145*, 115–119. https://doi.org/10.1016/j.socscimed.2015.09.020

Luken, M., & Sammons, A. (2016). Systematic review of mindfulness practice for reducing job burnout. *The American Journal of Occupational Therapy*, 70(2), 7002250020p1-7002250020p10. https://doi.org/10.5014/ajot.2016.016956

Malchiodi, C. A. (2007). *The art therapy sourcebook* (2nd ed.). New

York, NY: McGraw-Hill.

McCraty, R. (2015). *Science of the heart: Exploring the role of the human heart in human performance* (vol. 2). Boulder Creek, CA: HeartMath Institute.

McKay, M., & Fanning, P. (2000). *Self-esteem: A proven program of cognitive techniques for assessing, improving, & maintaining your self-esteem* (3rd ed.). Oakland, CA: New Harbinger Publications, Inc.

Meijer, D., & Geesink, H. (2017). Consciousness in the universe is scale invariant and implies an event horizon of the human brain. *NeuroQuantology* (September 2017) 153, pp. 15, 41-79. https://doi.org/10.14704/nq.2017.15.3.1079

Miller, A. I. (2000). *Insights of genius: Imagery and creativity in science and art.* Cambridge, MA: MIT Press.

Mishlove, J. (2000). *The PK man: A true story of mind over matter.* Charlottesville, VA: Hampton Roads Publishing Company, Inc.

Mishlove, J. (1988). *Psi development systems: The essential guide to psi phenomena from ancient origins to modern scientific evidence.* New York, NY: Ballantine Books.

Mishlove, J. (1993). *The roots of consciousness: The classic encyclopedia of consciousness studies revised and expanded* (revised ed.). New York, NY: Marlow & Company.

Mist, S. D., Aickin, M., Kalnins, P., Cleaver, J., Batchelor, R., Thorne, T., . . . Colbert, A. P. (2011). Reliability of AcuGraph system for measuring skin conductance at acupoints. *Acupuncture in Medicine*, 29(3), 221–226. https://doi.org/10.1136/aim.2010.003012

Moody, R. A. (2015). *Life after life: The bestselling original investigation that revealed "near-death experiences."* (Anniversary, special ed.). New York, NY: HarperOne.

Myers, D. G. (2002). *Intuition: Its powers and perils.* New Haven, CT: Yale University Press.

Neff, K. D. (2011). Self-compassion, self-esteem, and well-being. *Social and Personality Psychology Compass*, 5(1), 1–12. https://doi.org/10.1111/j.1751-9004.2010.00330.x

Nielsen, J. A., Zielinski, B. A., Ferguson, M. A., Lainhart, J. E., & Anderson, J. S. (2013). An evaluation of the left-brain vs. right-brain hypothesis with resting state functional connectivity magnetic resonance imaging. *PloS One*, 8(8), e71275. https://doi.org/10.1371/journal.pone.0071275

Parker, J., & Parker, D. (2001). *Parkers' astrology: The essential guide to using astrology in your daily life.* New York, NY: A Dorling Kindersley Publishing Book.

Pert, C. B. (1997). *Molecules of emotion.* New York, NY: Scribner.

Petervari, J., Osman, M., & Bhattacharya, J. (2016). The role of intuition in the generation and evaluation stages of creativity. *Frontiers in Psychology*, 7, 1420. https://doi.org/10.3389/fpsyg.2016.01420

Radin, D. (2013). *Supernormal: Science, yoga, and the evidence for extraordinary psychic abilities* (1st ed.). New York, NY: Deepak Chopra Books.

Radin, D. (2018). *Real magic: Ancient wisdom, modern science, and a guide to the secret power of the universe* (1st ed.). New York, NY: Harmony Books.

Remmers, C., & Zander, T. (2018). Why you don't see the forest for the trees when you are anxious: Anxiety impairs intuitive decision making. *Clinical Psychological Science*, 6(1), 48–62. https://doi.org/10.1177/2167702617728705

Rossman, M. (2011). *The worry solution: Using breakthrough brain science to turn stress and anxiety into confidence and happiness.* London: Rider Books.

Ruskan, J. (2003). *Emotional clearing: An east/west guide to releasing negative feelings and awakening unconditional happiness* (3rd ed.). New York, NY: R. Wyler & Co.

Sansone, R. A., & Sansone, L. A. (2010). Gratitude and well being: The benefits of appreciation. *Psychiatry* (Edgmont Township, PA), 7(11), 18–22.

Schmid, A. A., & van Puymbroeck, M. (2019). *Yoga therapy for stroke: A handbook for yoga therapists and healthcare professionals.* Philadelphia, PA: Singing Dragon Publishers.

Stahl, B., Goldstein, E., & Santorelli, S. (2010). *A mindfulness-based stress reduction workbook* (workbook ed.). Oakland, CA: New Harbinger Publications.

Strecher, V. J. (2016). *Life on purpose: How living for what matters most changes everything* (1st ed.). New York, NY: HarperOne.

Tigunait, P. R. (2018). *Sakti: A scholarly approach.* Retrieved from http://public.ebookcentral.proquest.com/choice/publicfullrecord.aspx?p=5490687

von Petzinger, G. (2016). *The first signs: Unlocking the mysteries of the world's oldest symbols* (reprint ed.). New York, NY: Atria Books.

Wallis, C. (2005, January 9). The new science of happiness. *Time.* Retrieved May 23, 2018, from http://content.time.com/time/magazine/article/0,9171,1015832-1,00.html

Wing, R. L. (1979). *The I Ching workbook* (1st ed.). Garden City, NY: Doubleday.

Woodyard, C. (2011). Exploring the therapeutic effects of yoga and its ability to increase quality of life. *International Journal of Yoga*, 4(2), 49–54. https://doi.org/10.4103/0973-6131.85485

Youssef, N. A., Lockwood, L., Su, S., Hao, G., & Rutten, B. P. F. (2018). The effects of trauma, with or without PTSD, on the transgenerational DNA methylation alterations in human off-springs. *Brain Sciences*, 8(5). https://doi.org/10.3390/brainsci8050083

Acknowledgements

I want to thank all of my teachers who have taught me how to listen to and trust my intuition, especially Betty Ann Ertwine. You have given me one of the greatest gifts. You have taught me how to listen and feel deeply! Thank you to my Heart Group: Paula Flom and Naomi Kimball guided by Betty Ann Ertwine, for endless, fun, love, and disciplined hours of meditating and practicing listening to our intuition with each other and seeing how what we intended and discovered would in fact unfold over the years.

Thank you to Jeffrey Mishlove for writing a beautiful and supportive foreword for this book, and for keeping the conversations going that validate the field of parapsychology and intuitive phenomena. Thank you to Russell DesMarais for initially teaching me how to meditate and cultivate energy for health and wellness with qigong and opening my mind and path to holistic health. Thank you to Susan Ezra and Terry Reed for teaching me guided imagery. Thank you to Pamela Eakins for teaching me the Kabbalah. Thank you to all of my teachers who have taught me various forms of healing. There are more of you than I can list here.

Thank you to all of the people I have had the honor to serve in healing sessions and classes. You have all taught me how to refine my skills and share the best way to listen to and trust your intuition.

Thank you to my editor, Betsy Robinson, for supporting me along the way, believing in my message, and helping me cut my teeth on my first book. Thank you to my copy editor, Mary Neighbour, for your thoroughness, and guiding me through the final steps, and helping me birth my book into the world. Thank you to Tauni Malmgren for your loyalty and assistance organizing references.

Thank you to Dan Eisner, Donald Empson, Christine Gendreau, Paula Flom, Betty Ann Ertwine, Nicole Hoekstra-Voves, Naomi Kimball, Victoria McCurdy, and Kari Rise for reading my manuscript, giving me invaluable feedback, and all of your encouragement. Thank you to all of my friends for your love and intuitive, spiritual, and healing discussions, and keeping me well, including Cliff Odendahl and

James Ryan. Additionally, thank you to my occupational therapy friends for your professional support: Rebecca Austill-Clausen, Michelle Bradshaw, Peggy Cherry, Ana Hernando, Mandy Lubas, Janell McClure, Betsy Shandalov, and Christina Spaeth-Harrer.

Thank you to my family: My mom, Kathleen Vadnais, who taught me how to have an open heart and mind, who learned hypnotherapy for my birth, and who I listened to type for hours while she ran a local newspaper and magazine for environmentally friendly publications. Thank you also for teaching me how to write beyond what I was taught in school. To my dad, John Vadnais, thank you for being the first to teach me relaxation techniques and opening me to the spiritual world, for sharing your past-life stories, and guiding us children to practice our telepathy. Thank you to my step-father, Donald Empson, for advising me to look up words when I was a kid, and being an excellent role model, along with my mother, and for giving me the other half of my writing gene. To my mother-in-law, Sally Dixon, thank you for encouraging me to follow what called me in life when I didn't feel I fit anywhere in mainstream healthcare. Thank you to my brothers and their families for always being there for me as a positive and connected force—Stephen Vadnais, Erik Vadnais, Joel Vadnais, and Scott Vadnais. To my husband, Alexander "Zander" Dixon, thank you, for loving and caring for me just the way I am and giving me time and space to pursue my interests and love.

I am grateful!

Heart Group, 2004 (L-R): Emmy Vadnais,
Betty Ann Ertwine, Paula Flom, and Naomi Kimball

Index

References are to page numbers. Figures and tables are identified as (fig.) or (tab.), respectively.

qigong: 94–95

quantum physics: 25–26, 35, 89
    See also quantum mechanics

reiki: 94, 97, 144,
    Small Universe Meditation:
    100

universal life energy: 27

yin and yang: 95, 100, 113

enlightenment: 15, 66, 114, 176

F

faith
    faith factor: 178–179
    prayer and: 144
    self-esteem and: 16

fear
    freedom from: 17–18
    guided imagery and: 85
    healing emotions: 147
    meditation and: 53
    nocebo: 150–152, 184–185
    See also stress

flow: 5, 15, 48
    energy and: 90–91, 93–95
    See also relaxation

focus: 17–18
    See also attention
    See also intention and
    manifestation

free will. *See* destiny and free will

G

Gach, Michael R., *Acupressure for
Emotional Healing: A Self-Care Guide
for Trauma, Stress, and Common
Emotional Imbalances*: 94, 221

genes. *See* DNA; Benson-Henry
Protocol

genetic expression: 54
    relaxation and: 16, 54–55, 59,
    74

gifts, spiritual: 171–172

goals. *See also* attention; beliefs;
clarity; focus; intention and
manifestation

goal setting: 138–139
    outcomes: 13–14, 139–140, 144
    unintended outcomes: 158–159
    vision board: 145–146

God. *See* higher power

gratitude: 13, 17–18
    emotion and: 147–148
    kindness and: 17
    Open Heart Meditation: 37–38
    Quick Coherence Technique: 35

Greenberg, Jerrold S. *Comprehensive
Stress Management*: 61, 199, 221

grief, loss, and healing
    guided imagery and: 85
    intuition and: 42, 160
    meditation benefits: 60
    normal reaction: 18
    spirituality
        heal and to connect with spiri-
        tuality: 171
        hunger: 169
        spiritual communication: 181
    See also depression; intu-
    ition-benefits of; stress; be-
    liefs-transforming expectations

grounding: 96–97
    Small Universe Meditation:
    101–102

guidance: 3, 19, 51, 69, 174, 185
    intuitive cards: 124
    messages and: 46
    See also decision-making;
    discernment

guided imagery: 132–133
    Inner Wisdom Guided Imagery
    (meditation): 88
    Special Place Guided Imagery
    (meditation): 87
    Working with an Image (guided
    imagery): 132–133
    See also imagination

About the Author

Emmy Vadnais, OTR/L, is an Occupational Therapist, Intuitive Healer, Health Coach, teacher, consultant, and writer. She provides holistic and integrative healthcare and intuitive development education to healthcare practitioners and organizations. She is the founder of the Holistic OT Community and is in private practice in St. Paul, Minnesota.

Dear Reader

Thank you for reading my book and letting me share my heart with you. If you enjoyed this book and found it helpful, please consider writing a positive review on Amazon or anywhere the book is sold. I welcome your comments and hearing about how intuition has improved your life.

If you would like more information about ways to develop your intuition with individual support from me or upcoming classes or events, please visit my website at EmmyVadnais.com. An "Intuitive Development" playlist is available on my YouTube channel at https://www.youtube.com/user/EmmyVadnais.

With Gratitude,

Emmy

Ellen Schaefer, *The Universe Is Within*, 2020

CPSIA information can be obtained
at www.ICGtesting.com
Printed in the USA
FSHW020117131120
75756FS

9 781735 263205